GCSE WJEC Eduqas
English Language

WJEC Eduqas GCSE English Language is a real challenge, but this brilliant CGP book makes it a lot easier to handle — it's the ultimate all-in-one guide to the course.

Inside, you'll find clear explanations, exam-style texts and plenty of indispensable practice questions... there's even a full practice exam at the end of the book.

What's more, we've included in-depth advice for the final exams, including graded sample answers that show you exactly how to score the top marks!

How to access your free Online Edition

This book includes a free Online Edition to read on your PC, Mac or tablet. You'll just need to go to **cgpbooks.co.uk/extras** and enter this code:

By the way, this code only works for one person. If somebody else has used this book before you, they might have already claimed the Online Edition.

D1439558

Complete
Revision & Practice
Everything you need to pass the exams!

9030 00006 6995 6

Contents

Section Four — Writing: Creative and Non-Fiction

Section Five — Paper 1: Sample Exam and Graded Answers

Section Six — Paper 2: Sample Exam and Graded Answers

Section Seven — Practice Exams

Published by CGP

Editors:
Izzy Bowen
Eleanor Claringbold
Katya Parkes

With thanks to James Summersgill for the proofreading
and Ana Pungartnik for the copyright research.

Acknowledgements:

Letter on page 27 to Princess (later Queen) Victoria from King Leopold I of Belgium,
August 1832, from The Letters of Queen Victoria, Volume 1 (of 3), 1837-1843.

With thanks to Atlantic Books for permission to use the extract from JMG Le Clézio 'Desert' on pages 86-87.

With thanks to Ross Parry / Yorkshire Post for permission to use the article on page 100.

Text on page 101 'The County Unit in Educational Organization', by Lawton B. Evans,
from The Granite Monthly, A New Hampshire Magazine, Volume 11, 1896.

Article entitled 'What are friends for?' on page 121 © Copyright Guardian News & Media Ltd 2018.

LONDON BOROUGH OF WANDSWORTH	
9030 00006 6995 6	
Askews & Holts	18-Apr-2019
J428.007 JUNIOR NON-	£7.50
	WW19000688

ISBN: 978 1 78908 243 2

Clipart from Corel®
Printed by Elanders Ltd, Newcastle upon Tyne.

Based on the classic CGP style created by Richard Parsons.

Text, design, layout and original illustrations © Coordination Group Publications Ltd. (CGP) 2019
All rights reserved.

Photocopying more than one section of this book is not permitted, even if you have a CLA licence.
Extra copies are available from CGP with next day delivery • 0800 1712 712 • www.cgpbooks.co.uk

Exam Structure

Understanding the structure of your exams is really important. You need to know what to expect on the day.

You will sit **Two** different exam papers

1) Your GCSE in English Language will be examined over <u>two</u> separate exam papers.
   <u>Paper 1</u> (or 'component 1') focuses on <u>fiction</u>, and <u>paper 2</u> (or 'component 2') focuses on <u>non-fiction</u>.

2) Both papers are split into <u>two</u> sections:

   • <u>Section A</u> contains <u>reading</u> questions, which test your ability to <u>understand</u> and <u>analyse</u> texts.

   • <u>Section B</u> tests your ability to <u>write</u> texts <u>of your own</u>.

Read the source texts **Carefully**

For <u>paper 1</u>, there will be a question paper, <u>one</u> extract from a work of literary fiction from the <u>20th century</u> and a separate answer book. You will have <u>1 hour 45 minutes</u> to complete this paper.

Section A (reading) will usually be made up of <u>5 questions</u> that are worth a total of <u>40 marks</u>.

• You should spend about <u>10 minutes</u> reading through the text and the questions, then about <u>50 minutes</u> writing your answers.

See p.2 for more about the assessment objectives.

• You'll be tested on <u>assessment objectives 1, 2 and 4</u> in this section.

Section B (writing) is worth <u>40 marks</u>. There'll be a <u>choice</u> of tasks, but you only need to do <u>one</u>.

• For this task, you should spend about <u>10 minutes</u> planning and <u>35 minutes</u> writing.

• You'll be tested on <u>assessment objectives 5 and 6</u> in this section.

For <u>paper 2</u>, there will be a question paper, <u>two</u> non-fiction sources — one from the <u>19th century</u> and one from the <u>21st century</u> — and a separate answer book. You will have <u>2 hours</u> to complete this paper.

If you have any time left at the end of the exam, use it to check through your work.

Section A (reading) will usually have <u>6 questions</u> that are worth a total of <u>40 marks</u>.

• You should spend about <u>10 minutes</u> reading through the texts and the questions, then about <u>50 minutes</u> writing your answers.

• You'll be tested on <u>assessment objectives 1, 2, 3 and 4</u> in this section.

Section B (writing) has two questions, worth <u>20 marks</u> each. You need to answer <u>both</u> questions:

• You should spend about <u>30 minutes</u> on each question.

• For each question, give yourself <u>5 minutes</u> to plan and <u>25 minutes</u> to write your answer.

• This section will test <u>assessment objectives 5 and 6</u>.

Both papers have the <u>same number</u> of marks, but paper 1 is worth <u>40%</u> of the GCSE and paper 2 is worth <u>60%</u>.

You need to know what each paper is going to look like...

After the reading time, you've got just over a minute per mark for the reading questions on both exam papers. If you keep to this rule you'll be able to attempt all the questions in the time you've been given.

The Assessment Objectives

If you've understood the basic structure of the exams, it's time to think about what the examiners are looking for in your answers. First, here's the background to what the questions are about — the assessment objectives.

Each **Assessment Objective** refers to a different **Skill**

1) The <u>assessment objectives</u> are the things that <u>Eduqas</u> say you need to <u>do</u> to get good marks in the exam.

2) They'll come in handy when you're working out what you need to do for <u>each question</u> (have a look back at p.1 to see which sections of the exams test which assessment objectives).

3) These exams test <u>assessment objectives 1 to 6</u>. Here's a brief description of each of them:

Assessment Objective 1

- <u>Pick out</u> and <u>understand</u> pieces of <u>explicit</u> and <u>implicit</u> information from the texts.

- <u>Collect</u> and <u>put together</u> information from different texts.

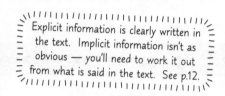
Explicit information is clearly written in the text. Implicit information isn't as obvious — you'll need to work it out from what is said in the text. See p.12.

Assessment Objective 2

- <u>Explain</u> how writers use <u>language</u> and <u>structure</u> to achieve their <u>purpose</u> and <u>influence</u> readers.

- Use <u>technical terms</u> to support your analysis of language and structure.

Assessment Objective 3

- <u>Identify</u> different writers' <u>ideas</u> and <u>perspectives</u>.

- <u>Compare</u> the <u>methods</u> used by different writers to convey their ideas.

Assessment Objective 4

- <u>Critically evaluate</u> texts, giving a <u>personal opinion</u> about how successful the writing is.

- Provide detailed <u>evidence</u> from the text to <u>support</u> your opinion.

Assessment Objective 5

- Write <u>clearly</u> and <u>imaginatively</u>, adapting your tone and style for various <u>purposes</u> and <u>audiences</u>.

- <u>Organise</u> your writing into a clear <u>structure</u>.

Assessment Objective 6

- Use a wide variety of <u>sentence structures</u> and <u>vocabulary</u>, so that your writing is <u>clear</u> and <u>purposeful</u>.

- Write <u>accurately</u>, paying particular attention to spelling, punctuation and grammar.

Remember what the examiner is looking for...

These assessment objectives are the basis for the exams (and their mark schemes), so it's really important that you get to know them. Try to keep them in mind when you're revising and writing exam answers.

Planning Answers

Now you know what the questions are focused on, the next few pages will help you to answer them.

Read the questions Carefully and Calmly

1) You should start each exam by spending about <u>10 minutes</u> reading through the <u>questions</u> and the <u>texts</u> in section A.

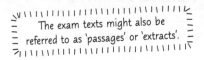
The exam texts might also be referred to as 'passages' or 'extracts'.

2) Always <u>read the questions</u> before the exam texts — that way, you'll know what to look out for.

3) Make sure you're clear about what the questions are <u>asking</u> you to do by <u>underlining</u> the <u>key words</u>.

| 1 | 5 | According to these <u>two writers</u>, <u>why</u> should people try to <u>spend less</u>? |

PAPER 2

4) Once you've read the questions, carefully <u>read</u> through the <u>texts</u>. It's a good idea to <u>highlight</u> key <u>words</u> or <u>phrases</u> in the texts that will help you to answer the questions — but don't spend ages doing this.

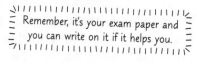
Remember, it's your exam paper and you can write on it if it helps you.

Jot down your Main Ideas before you start writing

1) Don't spend <u>too much</u> time planning. You don't need to write plans for the section A <u>reading</u> questions, though it might help to quickly jot down some <u>points</u> and <u>highlight</u> the texts.

2) You <u>should</u> do plans for the section B <u>writing</u> questions on both papers.

3) Don't go into too much <u>detail</u> — just get your <u>main ideas</u> down, and <u>outline</u> the <u>structure</u> of your answer.

| 2 | 2 | This is a statement made in an article that you have read: 'Modern music glorifies violent and criminal lifestyles and should be banned.' Write a speech, to be delivered in your school assembly, in which you explain your point of view on this statement. |

PAPER 2

<u>PLAN</u>

Make sure your points are linked to the question — think about purpose, form and audience.

Para 1 — Intro

    "My fellow students" etc, don't listen to critics — we're currently in golden era of music.

Para 2 — Not all modern music glorifies violence — give examples.

Para 3 — It's not just modern music — old music did this too. Give examples.

Para 4 — People aren't robots — won't just become violent by listening to music.

Para 5 — Ban = bad for freedom of expression. Censorship. Slippery slope etc.

Para 6 — Conc

    Critics = out of touch. Haven't listened to much 'modern music'.

    Modern music = celebration of choice.

Briefly outline the focus of each paragraph.

Make sure you're clear about which side you're arguing for before you start.

To save time, write in note form.

REVISION TASK

Planning can help focus your longer answers...

Have a go at making a brief plan for a creative writing story with the title 'The Dinner Party'. Note down your ideas about what might happen, and consider the structure of your answer too.

P.E.E.D.

To get good marks, you need to explain and develop your ideas properly. That's why P.E.E.D. is useful.

P.E.E.D. stands for **Point, Example, Explain, Develop**

To write good answers for the longer reading questions, you must do <u>four</u> things:

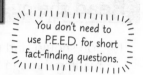
You don't need to use P.E.E.D. for short fact-finding questions.

1) Make a <u>point</u> to answer the question you've been given.

2) Then give an <u>example</u> from the text (see page 5 for more on this).

3) After that, <u>explain</u> how your example backs up your point.

4) Finally, <u>develop</u> your point — this might involve saying what the <u>effect on the reader</u> is, saying what the <u>writer's intention</u> is or <u>linking</u> your point to another part of the text.

The <u>explanation</u> and <u>development</u> parts are very important.
They're your chance to show that you <u>really understand</u> and
have <u>thought about</u> the text. Here are a couple of <u>examples</u>:

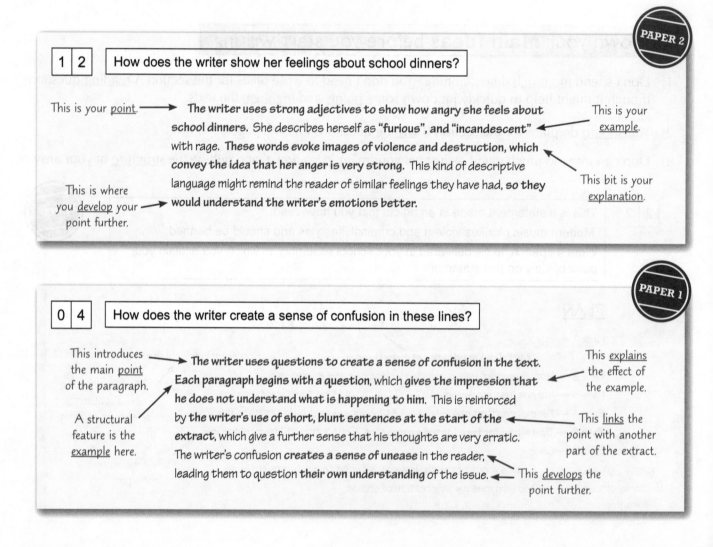

PAPER 2

| 1 | 2 | How does the writer show her feelings about school dinners?

This is your <u>point</u>. ——→ **The writer uses strong adjectives to show how angry she feels about school dinners. She describes herself as "furious", and "incandescent"** ←— This is your <u>example</u>.
with rage. These words evoke images of violence and destruction, which
convey the idea that her anger is very strong. This kind of descriptive
language might remind the reader of similar feelings they have had, **so they** — This bit is your <u>explanation</u>.

This is where you <u>develop</u> your point further. ——→ **would understand the writer's emotions better.**

PAPER 1

| 0 | 4 | How does the writer create a sense of confusion in these lines?

This introduces the main <u>point</u> of the paragraph. ——→ **The writer uses questions to create a sense of confusion in the text.**
Each paragraph begins with a question, which gives the impression that ←— This <u>explains</u> the effect of the example.
he does not understand what is happening to him. This is reinforced
by the writer's use of short, blunt sentences at the start of the ←— This <u>links</u> the point with another part of the extract.

A structural feature is the <u>example</u> here. ——→ **extract,** which give a further sense that his thoughts are very erratic.
The writer's confusion **creates a sense of unease in the reader,**
leading them to question **their own understanding of the issue.** ←— This <u>develops</u> the point further.

P.E.E.D. should help you to explain and develop your points...

Other versions of P.E.E.D. also focus on explaining and developing — P.E.E.R. (Point, Example, Explain, Relate), P.E.E.C.E. (Point, Example, Explain, Compare, Explore) and so on. Use the one you've been taught.

Using Examples

This page has some tips about the first 'E' in P.E.E.D. — giving examples to back up your points.

Use **Details** from the text to **Back Up** your points

1) Whenever you make a new <u>point</u>, you need to use short pieces of <u>evidence</u> from the text to <u>back it up</u>.

2) You should try to use a <u>mix</u> of different sorts of <u>evidence</u>.

3) If you're using <u>quotes</u>, try to keep them <u>short</u>. It'll really impress the examiner if you <u>embed</u> them in a sentence, like this:

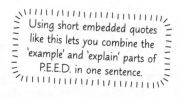
Using short embedded quotes like this lets you combine the 'example' and 'explain' parts of P.E.E.D. in one sentence.

> The writer refers to the situation as "indefensible", suggesting that he is extremely critical of the way it has been handled.

4) <u>Paraphrased details</u> from the text also work well as examples. You just need to describe one of the <u>writer's techniques</u>, or one of the <u>text's features</u>, in your own words, like this:

> The writer begins the paragraph with a rhetorical question that emphasises her feelings of disgust.

5) Here are a couple of <u>examples</u> to show you how to work your evidence into your answer:

PAPER 1

| 0 | 2 | How does the writer show the power of the fire? |

Embedding short quotes will help your answer to flow smoothly.

The writer uses a mixture of linguistic devices to demonstrate the immense power of the fire. At the start of the extract, he paints a vivid picture of the fire as a **"pageant"** of colour. He then **uses a metaphor to equate the destructive power of the fire with that of a beast** that is tearing down the workshop and **"devouring"** it. All of these images make the fire seem impressive and potent.

Your example could just be a description of one of the writer's techniques.

PAPER 2

| 1 | 6 | Both of these texts are about international travel. Compare the following: |

- the writers' attitudes to international travel;
- how they get across their arguments.

If you need to use a longer quote, make sure you copy it correctly and use the correct punctuation.

The author of the newspaper article has a very negative attitude towards international travel. In her opening paragraph, **she uses a long sentence** that is packed with negative verbs and adjectives, including **"delayed"** and **"dreary"**, to convey the hassle of long-distance travelling and to make the reader feel weary. By contrast, the author of the letter demonstrates a much more positive attitude. She opens her letter with the short but decisive sentence, **"The journey was a perfect joy!"**, which sounds energetic and cheerful.

Try to include a good balance of quotes and references to the text.

REVISION TIP

Make sure you're confident about using P.E.E.D....

It takes time to get used to using P.E.E.D. Try checking off the 'P', 'E', 'E' and 'D' in your mind (or even label them) when you write practice paragraphs. That way you'll find it easy in the exam.

Reading with Insight

To get the top grades, you need to show that you can 'read with insight' — you've got to make it clear that you understand more than just the obvious things. You can think of it as 'reading between the lines'.

You need to look **Beyond** what's **Obvious**

Looking beyond what's obvious will help you to make sure you've done the 'D' part of P.E.E.D. — look back at p.4 for more on this.

1) You may understand the <u>facts</u> a writer gives you, but you'll need to write about <u>more</u> than just those facts in your answers.

2) You can show <u>insight</u> if you work out what the writer's <u>intentions</u> are and how they want the reader to <u>feel</u>.

3) Here are a couple of <u>examples</u> of the kinds of things you could write:

> *The rhetorical questions make the reader doubt whether homework is a good thing. The writer seems to want to make readers feel guilty.*

 Think about the reasons <u>why</u> the writer has included certain features — show you've understood their <u>intended effect</u> on the reader.

> *There is a strong sense that the writer is suffering after the loss of his friend. Perhaps the writer felt he needed to make sure the memory of his friend was kept alive.*

You could comment on the writer's <u>attitude</u> and <u>why</u> you think they chose to write the piece.

Show you've thought about the **Writer's Intentions**

PAPER 1

| 0 | 5 |

"In the last nine lines of this passage, the writer encourages the reader to view Lilian as an unlikeable character."

To what extent do you agree with this view?

> Dylan glowered across the table at Lilian. She was composed and collected, her pointed, reptilian features gathered into an expression of infuriating complacency; as he watched, a smug smile flickered at the edges of her mouth. She knew she had won.
>
> There hadn't even been a discussion. Lilian had been cool and emotionless, the picture of relaxed indifference. Her cruel blow, calculated to achieve maximum damage with minimum effort, had been delivered with the sniper-like accuracy that Dylan had always known she was capable of. Reeling from the shock of her abrupt revelation, Dylan barely had time to collect himself before the others had arrived.

Always show how your interpretation is based on the text.

I agree that Lilian is portrayed as an unlikeable character in this extract. She is depicted as "smug" and she appears to be gloating. However, even though the writer is using the third-person, **he is still showing us Lilian from Dylan's perspective.** He has clearly been offended by her and so is biased against her. **Some readers might side with Dylan against Lilian,** finding her arrogant and malicious. **Having said that, other readers might** suspect that Dylan's pride has been wounded, and he is being overly harsh on Lilian as a result. **Personally, I think the writer is using this description of Lilian to influence** the reader's opinion of both her and Dylan by demonstrating that they both have flaws.

Try to pick out how the writer has made you feel like this.

Try to offer an alternative interpretation that goes beyond what is obvious in the text.

Show you've thought about what the writer is trying to achieve beyond the obvious.

Reading with Insight

Inference means working things out from Clues

1) Writers don't usually make things obvious — but you can use <u>evidence</u> from the text to make an <u>inference</u> about what the writer <u>really</u> wants us to think.

2) You need to analyse <u>details</u> from the text to show what they <u>reveal</u> about the writer's intentions:

> *The writer uses words like "endless" and "unoriginal", which imply that he did not enjoy the film.*   The writer's <u>language</u> indicates their <u>emotions</u> and <u>attitude</u>.

> *The writer sounds sarcastic when she calls the contestants "the finest brains the country could scrape together".*   The writer will often use <u>tone</u> (see page 32) to <u>imply</u> what they really mean — look out for <u>sarcasm</u> or <u>bias</u>.

3) You could use <u>phrases</u> like these to show that you've made an <u>inference</u>:

> The writer gives a sense of...

> The writer appears to be...

> This suggests that...

Try to Read Between the Lines

| 1 | 2 | How does the writer try to persuade us that the Internet has had a negative impact on our lives? |

> In today's world we are plagued by information. Gone are the days of blissful ignorance; instead we inhabit an era of awareness, where the invention of the Internet has brought the sum total of the world's knowledge to our fingertips. We are gluttons for information, and yet the immediate availability of this information has irrevocably extinguished the dying embers of our curiosity. No longer do we wonder about anything, we simply look it up. I am willing to concede that the Internet might be one of man's greatest inventions, but hey, so was the atomic bomb.

Analyse the writer's individual word choices for clues about how they try to affect the reader (see pages 34-35).

Writers often use sarcasm to try to persuade the reader to agree with them (see page 43).

The writer makes some **seemingly positive** claims about the Internet: she grandly asserts that it has created "an era of awareness" that has brought all the world's knowledge "to our fingertips". **However, the tone of the text suggests** that she wants the reader to see this as a bad thing. She uses negative words like **"plagued"** and **"gluttons"** to make the availability of information seem dangerous and excessive. She also describes the Internet as "one of man's greatest inventions", but the subsequent comparison to "the atomic bomb" indicates her **sarcastic tone**, and invites the reader to view the invention of the Internet as a destructive event.

Use words like 'seemingly' to show that you've thought about the meaning of the text beyond the obvious.

Your inferences could be based on the general feeling you get from reading the text.

Think about the effect the writer wants to create...

Everything in a text has been carefully crafted by the writer, so look for clues that reveal their intentions. Demonstrate that you understand what the writer is showing you, not just what they're telling you.

Writing Well

In these exams, it's not just what you write that's important — it's how you write as well.

Keep your writing **Formal** but **Interesting**

1) For these exams, it's important that you write in Standard English.

2) Standard English is the version of English that most people think is 'correct'. There are a few simple rules that you can follow to make sure you're writing in Standard English:

- Avoid using informal words and phrases (e.g. putting 'like' after sentences).
- Avoid using slang or local dialect words that some people might not understand.
- Use correct spelling, punctuation and grammar (have a look at pages 9-10).

Use clear **Explaining Words** and **Phrases**

1) You should use explaining words and phrases to make your answers easy to follow.

- This signifies that...
- This is reminiscent of...
- This highlights the fact that...
- Furthermore...
- This imagery reflects...
- This continues the idea of...

2) Using words and phrases like these makes your writing sound more professional.

3) They're also really useful when it comes to P.E.E.D. (see page 4). They help you to link the explanation and development parts of your answer to your main point.

Use **Paragraphs** to structure your answer

1) Your points need to be clearly organised and linked together. To do that you need to write in paragraphs.

2) You can use different paragraph structures to organise your points in different ways. For example:

- You could write a paragraph for every point you want to make, and each paragraph could have a P.E.E.D. structure (see page 4).
- You could make two points that contrast or agree with each other within a paragraph — this can be useful when comparing two texts.
- You could make one point and link together lots of examples with different explanations within a paragraph.

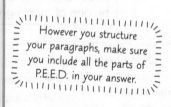

However you structure your paragraphs, make sure you include all the parts of P.E.E.D. in your answer.

3) Linking your paragraphs together smoothly makes your writing sound confident and considered. You could use linking words like these to help you do this:

- However...
- In the same way...
- In contrast...
- In addition...
- On the other hand...
- Alternatively...
- Equally...
- Conversely...

Your answer needs to have a clear structure...

Organise your ideas into paragraphs, and use the phrases to this page to link them together smoothly.
A clear structure will show the examiner that you've thought about your answer, and make it easier to read.

Spelling, Punctuation and Grammar

There are lots of marks available in these exams for correct use of spelling, punctuation and grammar, or SPaG for short. These pages should help you to avoid the most common SPaG errors...

SPaG is **Especially Important** for the **Writing** questions

1) It's important that you use correct spelling, punctuation and grammar in all of your answers.

2) However, it's particularly important for the writing questions (section B on both papers), as they will test your ability to write accurately and clearly — which includes good SPaG.

3) Here are some tips to help keep your writing as accurate as possible.

Spelling

1) Avoid common spelling mistakes, like 'their', 'they're' and 'there' or 'where', 'were' and 'wear'.

2) Remember that 'affect' is a verb, e.g. 'the simile affects the mood of the text', but 'effect' is a noun, e.g. 'the interruption has a shocking effect on the reader'.

3) Always write words out in full — avoid abbreviations like 'etc.' and 'e.g.', and don't use text speak.

4) Make sure any technical terms, like 'metaphor' or 'onomatopoeia', are spelt correctly.

5) Make sure any information taken from the extract, such as the writer's name, is spelt correctly.

Punctuation

1) Make sure you've used full stops at the end of sentences and question marks at the end of questions.

2) Use commas to separate items in a list or when you've used more than one adjective.

3) Use a comma when you use a joining word like 'and', 'so' or 'but' to link two points together. E.g. 'Jeremy says he isn't bothered by Mandy's behaviour, but his body language suggests otherwise.'

4) You should also use a pair of commas to separate extra information in a sentence. E.g. 'Ranjita, who is much calmer than Ashanti, does not respond to her father's taunting'.

5) Don't confuse colons and semi-colons:

- Colons can be used to introduce a list or if you want to add a piece of information that explains your sentence.

- Semi-colons can separate longer phrases in a list, or they can be used to join two sentences together — as long as both sentences are about the same thing and make sense on their own.

Grammar

1) Don't change tenses in your writing by mistake. If you're writing about a text in section A, always use the present tense, e.g. 'The writer uses alliteration to make Jane seem angry'.

2) Don't use double negatives, e.g. 'There wasn't no reason' should be 'There wasn't any reason'.

3) Remember 'it's' (with an apostrophe) is short for 'it is' or 'it has'. 'Its' (without an apostrophe) means 'belonging to it', e.g. 'The dog found its bone'.

4) Never write 'should of' — it's always 'should have', 'would have', 'could have'.

5) Start a new paragraph for each new point. Show that it's a new paragraph by starting a new line and leaving a gap or indent before you start writing.

Spelling, Punctuation and Grammar

Check over your Work when you've finished

1) Try to leave a few minutes at the <u>end</u> of the exams to <u>check</u> your work.

2) There might not be <u>time</u> to check everything thoroughly. Look for the <u>most obvious</u> spelling, punctuation and grammar mistakes.

3) Start by checking your answers to the <u>writing questions</u> (section B on both papers), as these are the ones where you get the <u>most marks</u> for accuracy.

4) Here are some tips for <u>correcting</u> any mistakes that you find:

- If you find a <u>spelling mistake</u>, put <u>brackets</u> around the word, <u>cross it out</u> neatly with <u>two lines</u> through it and write the correction <u>above</u>.

- If you've written something which isn't clear, put an <u>asterisk</u> (*) at the end of the sentence. Put another asterisk at the end of your work, and write what you mean beside it.

- If you realise you should have started a <u>new paragraph</u>, put // to show where it <u>starts</u> and write "(para)" in the margin.

- If you find you've <u>missed out</u> a word or two, put a "∧" where the words should go, then write them in <u>above</u> the line.

Make corrections as Neatly as possible

PAPER 1

SECTION B: WRITING

1 1   (a) Write a story which begins: *The air was stiflingly hot...*

Make sure you use semi-colons and colons correctly.

The air was stiflingly hot. Sunita could feel a **dewy coating** of sweat materialising on her **clammy** skin as she ∧ in the middle of the park. She kept one eye on the romantic novel that she held in her hand, and the other peering through the summer haze at Ollie as he charged around the open space with the other boys. It was difficult to concentrate on anything in this **weather; Sunita** had felt harassed and tormented by the **relentless, sweltering** heat all week. // Her mind wandered from the **novel,** **and she began** to ponder the evening ahead. **She had** originally planned to wear her comfortable but contemporary denim skirt with her favourite brown boots. This was certainly not an option in this weather though. She would have to think of something else. Perhaps the floral dress that **she had worn** last summer to Rachel's wedding would work.

    Suddenly, her rambling mind was brought back to reality with a start. A loud scream resonated around the park. Sunita jumped to her (feat) and began running.

reclined (inserted above "as she")

(para)

feet (correction above "feat")

Commas can be used between two adjectives or before a joining word that is being used to link two points.

Think carefully about how you link your paragraphs.

Accuracy is important, but don't let it put you off using a wide range of vocabulary and sentence structures.

Be careful with your tenses — make sure they're consistent.

Correct any mistakes clearly and neatly.

Make sure you can spell some more complex words...

EXAM TIP

You should use a wide range of vocabulary and sentence types in your writing, but you also need to use these correctly, with accurate SPaG. Try to find a balance between accuracy and imagination.

Revision Summary

At the end of most sections in this book, you'll find pages like this one. They're important, so don't skip them.

You've read the section, but do you know it? Here's where you find out — right here, right now.

- Try these questions and <u>tick off each one</u> when you <u>get it right</u>.
- When you've done <u>all the questions</u> under a heading and are <u>completely happy</u> with it, tick it off.

Planning, P.E.E.D. and Using Examples (p.3-5) ☑

1) True or false?
   You should make a detailed plan for every question in these exams. ☑

2) What does P.E.E.D. stand for? ☑

3) Give three ways that you could develop a point. ☑

4) In your longer answers, how many of your points should be backed up with evidence
   from the text?
   a) A few of them
   b) About half of them
   c) Some of them
   d) All of them ☑

5) Write down two different types of evidence that you could give from a text. ☑

Reading with Insight and Writing Well (p.6-8) ☑

6) Give two examples of things you could comment on to show that you are reading with insight. ☑

7) What does 'inference' mean? ☑

8) Give an example of a phrase you could use to show that you've made an inference. ☑

9) Which of these words and phrases could you use to link paragraphs in an exam answer?
   a) secondly   b) safe to say   c) in addition to this   d) conversely ☑

Spelling, Punctuation and Grammar (p.9-10) ☑

10) Which of the following sentences is correct?
    a) I think the writer's use of metaphors in this extract is very effective.
    b) I think the writer's use of metaphors in this extract is very affective. ☑

11) Give three uses of commas. ☑

12) Does the following sentence use a semi-colon correctly?
    Gazing out of the open window; Tomek dreamt of the day when he would be free from revision. ☑

13) What is a double negative? ☑

14) Where is the grammatical error in the following sentence?
    You could of used a better paragraph structure to improve your answer. ☑

15) When checking your answers for SPaG errors, which ones should you check first? ☑

16) Write down the correction symbols for the following situations:
    a) When a new paragraph should start
    b) When a word or two is missing
    c) When something isn't clear ☑

Information and Ideas

These two pages will help you with assessment objective 1 (see p.2). This page is about picking out information from a text, and the next page is about summarising information from two different texts.

Information and ideas can be **Explicit** or **Implicit**

1) The first thing you need to be able to do in order to <u>analyse</u> a text is to <u>understand</u> the basic things it's <u>telling you</u>.

2) This will help you to pick up some <u>easy marks</u> for <u>section A</u> in both exam papers.

3) The information and ideas you need to pick out will either be <u>explicit</u> or <u>implicit</u>.

4) <u>Explicit</u> information is <u>clearly written</u> in the text.

Last weekend, it rained a lot.	The text states that it rained, so we <u>know</u> that it rained. We also know <u>how much</u> it rained — "a lot."

5) <u>Implicit</u> information needs a little more <u>detective work</u> — you'll need to work it out from what is said in the text.

The castle was dark, decrepit and freezing cold.	In this sentence, it is <u>implied</u> that the author doesn't like the castle very much, but this isn't stated outright.

Underline the **Relevant Facts** as you **Read** the text

PAPER 1

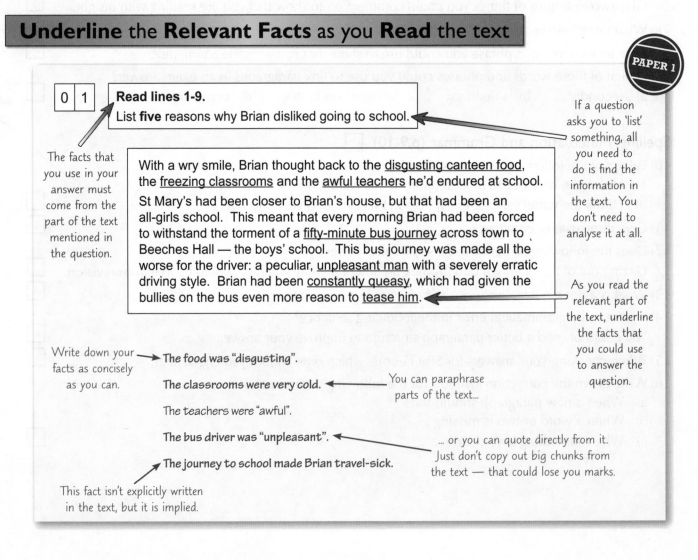

0 1   Read lines 1-9.
List **five** reasons why Brian disliked going to school.

The facts that you use in your answer must come from the part of the text mentioned in the question.

If a question asks you to 'list' something, all you need to do is find the information in the text. You don't need to analyse it at all.

With a wry smile, Brian thought back to the <u>disgusting canteen food</u>, the <u>freezing classrooms</u> and the <u>awful teachers</u> he'd endured at school.

St Mary's had been closer to Brian's house, but that had been an all-girls school. This meant that every morning Brian had been forced to withstand the torment of a <u>fifty-minute bus journey</u> across town to Beeches Hall — the boys' school. This bus journey was made all the worse for the driver: a peculiar, <u>unpleasant man</u> with a severely erratic driving style. Brian had been <u>constantly queasy</u>, which had given the bullies on the bus even more reason to <u>tease him</u>.

As you read the relevant part of the text, underline the facts that you could use to answer the question.

Write down your facts as concisely as you can.

The food was "disgusting".

The classrooms were very cold.

The teachers were "awful".

The bus driver was "unpleasant".

The journey to school made Brian travel-sick.

You can paraphrase parts of the text...

... or you can quote directly from it. Just don't copy out big chunks from the text — that could lose you marks.

This fact isn't explicitly written in the text, but it is implied.

Information and Ideas

You'll also need to **Summarise** information

1) In section A of paper 2, you will be asked to pick out information and ideas on the <u>same topic</u> from two <u>different texts</u>.

2) You then need to write a <u>summary</u> about the <u>topic</u> — a piece of writing that <u>combines</u> the ideas from both texts, but is written using your <u>own words</u>.

3) Summaries need to be <u>concise</u> — try to sum up <u>all</u> the information you've gathered in as <u>few sentences</u> as possible.

4) For summarising questions, you <u>don't</u> need to <u>compare</u> the two texts — you just need to <u>explain</u> what they say about the <u>topic</u> in the question.

5) Even though you're using your own words, you still need to <u>back up</u> everything you write with a range of <u>examples</u> from both texts.

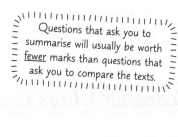

Questions that ask you to summarise will usually be worth <u>fewer</u> marks than questions that ask you to compare the texts.

Collect information from **Both** texts

PAPER 2

| 1 | 5 | According to these two writers, why should people avoid travelling? |

This question asks you to summarise what the texts say about why people shouldn't travel.

21st-century newspaper

In general, travelling is the last way I want to spend my time: the stress of catching connecting planes or trains gives me a coronary, and I suffer from chronic, restless boredom when forced to sit down for long periods of time. The environmental costs of travel also turn me off the idea — long-haul flights release tonnes of harmful carbon emissions into the atmosphere.

19th-century letter

The journey was simply dreadful, my dear Louisa. I know it is not becoming of a lady to say such things, but the jolting of the carriage has left my poor nerves shot to pieces; a truly alarming experience. And yet somehow so tedious, too — I should think that there is no activity more monotonous than the act of transporting oneself from one destination to another.

Combine evidence from both texts to make your answer as concise as possible.

The writers suggest that you should **avoid travelling** because it can be both stressful and monotonous: in the newspaper article, the writer mentions that journeys can involve "stress" and "boredom", and the writer of the letter mentions the effect of travel on her "nerves", as well as how "tedious" she finds travelling. **In the modern age, there are also environmental reasons not to travel**, as the writer of the newspaper article explains: long-haul flights release "**tonnes of harmful carbon emissions**" into the air.

Use key words to show the examiner that you've understood the question.

Answer the question in your own words, then back your points up with evidence from the texts.

Get used to picking out explicit and implicit information...

REVISION TASK

Read some newspaper articles and underline any information which is given explicitly. Then, look closely at the language and note down the implicit ideas that the writers have expressed too.

Audience

In the exams, you'll need to think about the audience — the intended readers of the text.

Writers aim their work at **General** or **Specific** audiences

1) The writer will always have a <u>group of people</u> in mind when they write — this is their <u>audience</u>.

2) The audience of a text can be quite <u>general</u>, e.g. adults, or more <u>specific</u>, e.g. parents with children under the age of 3.

3) Some texts will have <u>more than one</u> audience, e.g. children's books will try to appeal to the <u>kids</u> who read them, but also to the <u>parents</u> who will <u>buy</u> them.

Look for **Clues** about the target audience

1) Sometimes you can work out <u>who</u> the target audience is by the text's <u>content</u> (subject matter):

> *This latest model is a beautiful car. Its impressive engine can send you shooting from 0-60 mph in less than 8 seconds.*

This text is clearly aimed at someone who's interested in <u>high-performance cars</u>.

2) The <u>vocabulary</u> (choice of words) can tell you about the target audience, e.g. about the <u>age group</u>:

> *Today, we witnessed a discussion on fox hunting. As one can imagine, this issue, although it has been debated for many years, still managed to elicit mixed emotions from all concerned.*

The <u>sophisticated vocabulary</u>, like 'elicit', rather than 'bring out', and the <u>complex sentences</u> show that this text is aimed at <u>adults</u>.

> *Dungeon Killer 3 is the hottest new game of the year! There are 52 awesome levels and 6 cool new characters — don't miss out on the wildest gaming experience of your life!*

This one uses modern <u>slang</u> and <u>simple sentences</u>, so it's clear that this text is aimed at <u>younger people</u>.

3) The <u>language</u> can also give you clues about the target audience's <u>level of understanding</u>:

> *The object of a game of football is to get the ball in the opposing team's goal. Sounds easy, but the other team has the same thing in mind. Also, there are eleven players on the other team trying to stop you.*

The <u>simple</u>, <u>general</u> explanations in this text show that it's written for people who <u>don't know much</u> about football.

> *The next hole was a par 3 and I hit my tee shot directly onto the green. Sadly, my putting let me down badly, and I ended up getting a bogey.*

The <u>technical vocabulary</u> here shows that this is for people who know <u>quite a bit</u> about golf.

EXAM TIP

Work out a text's intended audience as soon as you can...

As you begin reading, identify the text's audience and keep it in mind throughout your answer. It'll help you to discuss the writer's purpose, the techniques they use and how successful they are.

Writer's Purpose

Every text you come across in your English Language exams will have been written for a reason.

There are **Four Common Purposes** of writing

1) The purpose of a text is the reason that it's been written — what the writer is trying to do.

2) Most texts are written for one of these reasons:

To Argue or Persuade
*   They give the writer's opinion.
*   They get the reader to agree with them.

To Advise
They help the reader to do something.

They give instructions on what to do.

To Inform
*   They tell the reader about something.
*   They help the reader to increase their understanding of a subject.

To Entertain
*   They are enjoyable to read.
*   They make the reader feel something.

3) Lots of texts have more than one purpose, though. E.g. a biographical text could be written to both inform and entertain its audience.

Pages 16-19 tell you how to spot a text's purpose, and how you can discuss this in the exams.

4) In the exams, read the texts carefully and make sure that you think about what the writers are trying to achieve (and how they're achieving it).

5) Look out for helpful exam questions that actually tell you the writer's purpose. E.g. if the question asks you about how the writer uses language to influence the reader, you know it's about persuading.

Purpose is **More Obvious** in **Non-fiction** texts

1) The purpose of most non-fiction texts is usually quite obvious. For example:

> If a speech is trying to argue a particular point of view, the writer might make this very clear to make the argument more powerful.

2) Look out for texts where it might be less obvious, though. For example:

> A magazine article is primarily written to entertain its audience, so it might use a chatty tone to engage the reader. This might make it less obvious that it's also trying to argue a particular point of view.

3) A piece of fiction's most obvious purpose is to entertain, but writers sometimes use entertainment to achieve another purpose.

> Lots of fiction texts are entertaining stories on the surface, but they can contain another message. The writer might want to argue their own point of view or inform the reader about something.

You need to know the writer's purpose to write a good answer...

Always make sure you consider a text's purpose. If there's more than one purpose to a text, write about them both. And if you can write about how one purpose is used to achieve another, that's even better.

Informative Texts

Informative texts (like this book, in fact) always have something they're trying to tell you.

Informative writing Tells you something

1) When writing an informative text, the writer's aim is to pass on <u>knowledge</u> to the reader as <u>clearly</u> and <u>effectively</u> as possible.

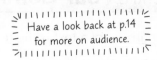
Have a look back at p.14 for more on audience.

2) They will adapt their <u>language</u> to match their intended <u>audience</u>, e.g. they <u>might</u> need to write for different <u>age groups</u>, or for people with different <u>levels of understanding</u>.

3) Purely informative texts will present information in a <u>balanced</u> and <u>factual</u> way. They will contain lots of <u>facts</u> and <u>figures</u>, but no <u>opinions</u>.

4) Some informative texts might also be <u>arguing</u> a particular viewpoint, though. For example:

> Many newspapers <u>carefully pick</u> information that supports a particular political party. Even though a newspaper article may not say outright what its opinion is, it can still be <u>biased</u>.

Bias is when a piece of writing is influenced by the opinion of its author — see page 45.

Read the passage Carefully

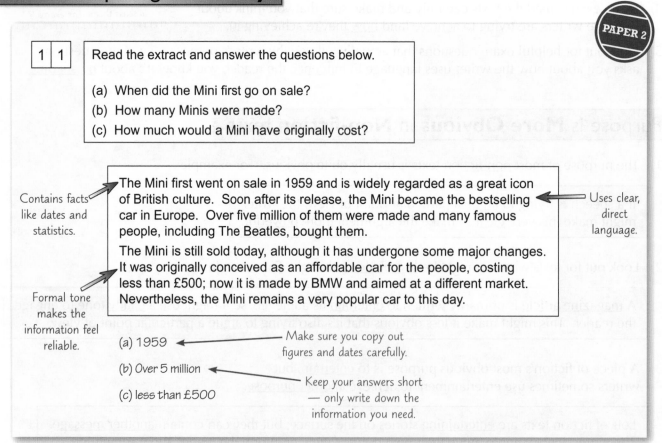

PAPER 2

| 1 | 1 | Read the extract and answer the questions below.

(a) When did the Mini first go on sale?
(b) How many Minis were made?
(c) How much would a Mini have originally cost?

Contains facts like dates and statistics.

The Mini first went on sale in 1959 and is widely regarded as a great icon of British culture. Soon after its release, the Mini became the bestselling car in Europe. Over five million of them were made and many famous people, including The Beatles, bought them.

The Mini is still sold today, although it has undergone some major changes. It was originally conceived as an affordable car for the people, costing less than £500; now it is made by BMW and aimed at a different market. Nevertheless, the Mini remains a very popular car to this day.

Uses clear, direct language.

Formal tone makes the information feel reliable.

(a) 1959

Make sure you copy out figures and dates carefully.

(b) Over 5 million

Keep your answers short — only write down the information you need.

(c) less than £500

Look at some examples of informative writing as practice...

You need to be able to recognise informative writing and explain how it's being used. If the information is biased, make sure you comment on that. It will show the examiner that you've really thought about the text.

Entertaining Texts

Entertaining texts make you feel something. You need to be able to explain how they do this.

Entertaining writing aims to be Enjoyable to read

1) Entertaining writing is the sort of thing you'd read for <u>pleasure</u>, e.g. literary fiction.

2) Unlike informative texts, they contain <u>few facts</u>. Instead, they try to make you <u>feel</u> something, like <u>scared</u>, <u>excited</u>, or <u>amused</u>.

3) Entertaining writing is often very <u>descriptive</u>, and uses <u>narrative techniques</u> to make texts more enjoyable to read (see p.46 and p.50).

4) Writers also use <u>structural techniques</u> to create entertaining texts (see p.51-55). E.g. lots of <u>short</u>, <u>punchy</u> sentences can be used to make a text feel more <u>exciting</u>.

> Writers might use entertaining writing to <u>engage</u> a reader when they have <u>another</u> purpose in mind. E.g. travel books are <u>entertaining non-fiction</u>, but they're also <u>informative</u>.

Think about What makes the text entertaining

PAPER 1

| 0 | 4 | How does the writer make these lines exciting and tense? |

Lots of creative vocabulary makes the text more interesting.

> He could feel the power of the bike humming beneath him as they both hurtled along. They were an elegant couple skimming the dance floor, whirling past plodding onlookers in their graceless automobiles, twisting around sweeping corners with effortless precision and darting along endless straights as they pushed each other on towards the inevitable conclusion. The bike hit the wall with all its hulking force.

The text uses imagery to make the description come to life.

Different sentence lengths give the text an interesting structure.

Use key words from the question to keep your answer focused.

You need to use technical terms.

In order to **build excitement for the reader**, the writer uses an extended **metaphor** that personifies the bike as a dance partner. The bike and the rider become an "elegant couple" whose movements contrast with the "**plodding**" cars. The writer uses a long sentence to develop this metaphor and build drama. This **lengthy second sentence** contains several verbs that are related to dancing and speed, such as "whirling" and "darting". The cumulative effect of these **verbs** makes the reader feel tense. It is as if the sentence is rushing and building towards a conclusion. **The writer then disperses this tension** with the final short sentence. The phrase "hit the wall" is very blunt, and contrasts to the preceding build-up, **adding to the shock and impact of the conclusion.**

You should analyse the language at both word and sentence level.

Try to identify how the writer uses different parts of speech.

Write about the writer's intentions and the effects of their language on the reader.

Many entertaining texts also have other purposes...

Entertaining writing really helps to keep readers interested. So even if a writer's main purpose is to inform, argue, persuade or advise, they might still want to make their writing entertaining so the reader enjoys it.

Texts that Argue or Persuade

When you're writing about a text that argues or persuades, you need to be able to say exactly how it does this.

Arguing and Persuading are Similar

1) When people write to <u>argue</u>, they want to make the reader <u>agree</u> with their <u>opinion</u>. They use <u>clear</u> and <u>forceful</u> language to get their points across, and they might use <u>facts and figures</u> to back up points.

2) <u>Persuasive</u> writing tries to get the reader to <u>do something</u>, such as support a charity. It does this with techniques including <u>emotive language</u> that aims to make the reader <u>sympathise</u> with their cause.

3) When writing to <u>persuade</u>, writers might sometimes be <u>more subtle</u> about their aims and opinions, e.g.:

> *It is clear that this is a good school, and that people who attend it do well.*

This writer uses the phrase 'It is clear' to make their <u>opinion</u> sound like <u>fact</u>. This can make the writing sound more <u>informative</u>, when actually it's <u>persuasive</u>.

4) When writing to argue or persuade, writers often use <u>rhetorical devices</u> such as <u>hyperbole</u>, <u>repetition</u> or <u>rhetorical questions</u> (see p.44).

Explain the Effects of the writer's choice of Language

PAPER 2

1 2 David Barowsky is trying to persuade us to eat breakfast. How does he try to do this?

WHY BOTHER WITH BREAKFAST?

David Barowsky, *nutritional analyst*

Eating breakfast improves mental and physical performance. This is a well-known and incontrovertible fact. And yet 20 million of us Britons regularly skip this essential refuelling opportunity. Why is this the case? Are we too busy commuting, getting the kids ready for school, blow-drying our hair? Do you often feel frantic and harassed in the morning? Well, the time has come to change your ways. Allowing your kids to skip breakfast is reckless and irresponsible. You are not providing them with the energy they need to face the day.

The writer uses statements to make their point clearly and forcefully.

Uses rhetorical questions.

Facts and figures are used to back up their argument.

Addresses the reader directly using the pronoun 'you'.

Try to use varied vocabulary to describe the effects of the writer's language on the reader.

The writer captures the reader's attention by using an **alliterative** rhetorical question as a title. Barowsky then immediately, and assertively, answers the question in the first line. This makes the writer sound both **authoritative** and **knowledgeable**, so readers are more likely to trust him and follow his advice to "bother with breakfast". Barowsky also uses the **personal pronouns** "you" and "we" to establish a connection with the reader, whilst powerful adjectives like **"reckless"** and **"irresponsible"** encourage an emotional response. This personal connection gives the writer a platform from which he can challenge the reader's actions and persuade them to agree with his views.

Try to use technical terms wherever you can.

Comment on the effects of individual words.

Consider how effective texts that argue or persuade are...
Whenever you're reading texts which argue or persuade, think about whether it convinces you to share the writer's point of view. How does it achieve its purpose, or why was it not successful?

Texts that Advise

When writing to advise, a writer uses reassuring and easily understandable language to guide their reader.

Writing to **Advise** sounds **Clear** and **Calm**

1) When writing to <u>advise</u>, writers want their readers to <u>follow their suggestions</u>.

2) The tone will be <u>calm</u> and <u>less emotional</u> than writing that argues or persuades.

3) The advice will usually be <u>clear</u> and <u>direct</u>. For example, it might use:

> • <u>Vocabulary</u> that matches the audience's <u>subject knowledge</u>.
> • <u>Second person</u> pronouns (e.g. 'you') to make the advice feel <u>personal</u>.
> • A <u>logical structure</u> that makes the advice <u>easy to follow</u>.

4) The register (see p.33) may be <u>formal</u>, e.g. in a letter from a solicitor offering legal advice, or <u>informal</u>, e.g. in a magazine advice column.

Writing to **Advise** looks **Like This**

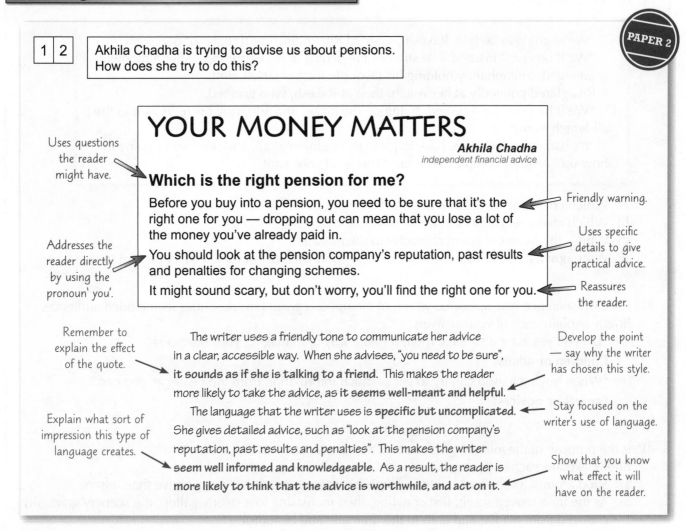

PAPER 2

| 1 | 2 | Akhila Chadha is trying to advise us about pensions. How does she try to do this? |

YOUR MONEY MATTERS

Akhila Chadha
independent financial advice

Which is the right pension for me?

Before you buy into a pension, you need to be sure that it's the right one for you — dropping out can mean that you lose a lot of the money you've already paid in.

You should look at the pension company's reputation, past results and penalties for changing schemes.

It might sound scary, but don't worry, you'll find the right one for you.

Uses questions the reader might have.

Addresses the reader directly by using the pronoun 'you'.

Friendly warning.

Uses specific details to give practical advice.

Reassures the reader.

Remember to explain the effect of the quote.

The writer uses a friendly tone to communicate her advice in a clear, accessible way. When she advises, "you need to be sure", **it sounds as if she is talking to a friend**. This makes the reader more likely to take the advice, as **it seems well-meant and helpful**.

The language that the writer uses is **specific but uncomplicated**. She gives detailed advice, such as "look at the pension company's reputation, past results and penalties". This makes the writer **seem well informed and knowledgeable**. As a result, the reader is **more likely to think that the advice is worthwhile, and act on it**.

Develop the point — say why the writer has chosen this style.

Stay focused on the writer's use of language.

Explain what sort of impression this type of language creates.

Show that you know what effect it will have on the reader.

REVISION TASK

Learn the common features of texts that advise...

Texts that advise often share key features. Make a checklist of these so that you can easily spot texts that advise in the exam. You could do this for each of the other common writing purposes.

Warm-Up Questions

To help you to digest everything you've read so far, here's a page of warm-up questions. They shouldn't take you too long, but try to write a few sentences for questions 3 and 4. You can check your answers in the back of the book to see how you're getting on. Then, when you're ready, have a look at page 21.

Warm-Up Questions

1) Read the short passage below.

> Dani approached the roller coaster with wide eyes. Her friend Amara had offered to give £20 to charity if Dani agreed to ride the biggest roller coaster in the park — a towering steel beast with four loops and six corkscrew turns. Her stomach churned at the thought.

Are the following statements true or false?
a) Dani is nervous about going on the roller coaster.
b) It was Dani's idea to get sponsored to go on the ride.

2) Read the short passage below.

> "We're going to be late, Rakesh," warned Rita, biting her thumbnail nervously.
> "We'll be fine!" insisted Rakesh from the depths of his wardrobe. After a moment he emerged, triumphantly holding his favourite leather jacket aloft.
> Rita glared pointedly at her watch, then at Rakesh, who grinned.
> "We'll be fine," he repeated, trying on the jacket and admiring his reflection in the full-length mirror.
> "It's bad enough that we have to go to this reunion at all, and now we're going to show up late too," complained Rita. "This is all your fault."

a) Which character is reluctant to go to the reunion?
b) Which character cares most about time management?
c) Who is the more confident character in the passage?
d) Write down a quote from the passage to support each of your answers to parts a) to c).

3) For each sentence below, decide which of the options given best describes its intended audience. Briefly explain each of your answers.
a) "Do you yearn for a simpler, more reliable way of managing your finances?"
   Children or adults?
b) "When buying a used car, try to get as much information from the dealer as you can."
   Experts or novices?

4) Is the purpose of the following sentences to entertain, persuade or advise? Briefly explain each of your answers.
a) Shop around for the best quote — some insurers are much more expensive than others.
b) As the train moved south, first crawling, then increasing to a steady gallop, the scenery gradually changed from the flat and drab to the dramatic and beautiful.
c) Who could disagree with the fact that children should eat healthily?

Exam-Style Questions

Now you've learnt some theory, it's time to put it into practice with these exam-style questions. They're very similar to the ones you'll see in the real Eduqas English Language exams. You should try to do them without looking back at this section for help. You can mark yourself using the answers in the back of the book.

Q1   Read the following extract from a novel.

List **five** facts from the text about George.

> The doorbell rang. Someone must have answered it, because moments later I heard George's nasal tones in the hallway.
> "So lovely to be here!" he cried, his voice carrying easily across the living room.
> "Did you invite him?" I hissed, staring desperately at Rosa.
> "I could hardly leave him out," she said coolly. "It would have been too obvious."
> He entered the room. His garish purple suit and elaborate hairstyle made him stand out sharply from the other guests. "George, darling," Rosa cooed. "You made it."
> "Rosa!" he said, presenting her with a bottle of cheap-looking wine. "And Freddie," he said to me with a smirk, extending a greasy hand adorned with several gaudy rings. "Good to see you."
> "You too," I said, forcing a smile and letting go of his hand quickly. "Drink?"
> "Oh, go on then," said George, "I'd love a nice whisky, if you have any?"
> "Nothing but the best for you, George," I replied through gritted teeth.

Q2   Read the following extracts.

> **19th-Century Letter**
> Dearest Jane,
>   I have just come to the end of a most fascinating novel. Increasingly, I find myself considering reading to be the most entertaining way to occupy oneself. I tire easily of needlework, and music bores me, but I could, and do, read on for hours and hours. I have learnt about many fascinating places that I could never hope to visit myself, all from my own little chair, or whilst travelling in my carriage.

> **21st-Century Newspaper Article**
>   Despite the waning popularity of reading amongst the younger generation, I think there's still something to be said for losing yourself in a good book. What other hobby can you do for hours on end without getting bored?
>   Long train journeys, beach holidays, cosy Sunday afternoons — it doesn't matter where you are, reading is always a convenient and enjoyable activity.
>   What's more, reading widens your horizons — I've learnt more from books than I ever did from my school teachers.

According to these two writers, why should people read books?

Exam-Style Questions

Q3 Read the following extract from a review of a holiday park, then answer the questions underneath.

> You would need a fortnight to try all the activities at Lowbridge Park. From abseiling to zorbing, the park offers a mind-boggling range of activities. I was only there for a long weekend, so I had to prioritise!
>
> I began with a pony trek. Although it drizzled the entire morning, it was a great way to explore the woodland. In the afternoon I debated between rock climbing and mountain biking. I settled on the former, primarily to stay out of the rain!
>
> The next day, the weather was better, so my choice fell between canoeing and sailing. I settled for a canoe and headed out on the lake, which was stunning early in the morning. The good weather lasted into the afternoon, which meant that I was also lucky enough to be able to go paragliding. What an exhilarating experience!
>
> I decided to finish my trip with a spot of archery. Alas, I'm no Robin Hood, but the instructor was patient, and I improved a little over the course of the morning.

a) How long does the writer think it would take to try everything at Lowbridge Park?

b) Why did the writer decide to go rock climbing?

c) What was the writer's final activity at the park?

Q4 Read the following extract from an advice leaflet about an election.

> ## It's Decision Time — But Who Do I Vote For?
>
> Unless you've been living under a rock for the past month, you'll probably have noticed that there's an election coming up. Deciding who to vote for can be a daunting task, but it's also an important one. Luckily, there's plenty of help out there.
>
> Firstly, you need to be well-informed on the principles and policies that each party stands for. If you start to feel overwhelmed by all the political lingo in their leaflets, don't panic — have a look online, where there are plenty of websites that break it down for you.
>
> It's also a good idea to look into the candidates in your constituency. They represent you in parliament, so you'll want to vote for someone who has a strong voice, and who will stand up for what your area needs.
>
> It's true — choosing who to vote for isn't easy. However, if you take the time to do a bit of research, you will be able to make the right decision for you.

The writer is trying to advise the reader about voting in an election.
How do they try to do this?

You should comment on:

- what they say to advise readers;
- their use of language, tone and structure;
- the way they present their ideas.

Writer's Viewpoint and Attitude

You always need to be aware of the writer's viewpoint, but it's especially important for paper 2.

Viewpoint and Attitude are Different to Purpose

1) A writer's purpose is what they're trying to <u>do</u>, but their <u>viewpoint</u> (or attitude) is what they <u>think</u> about the <u>topics</u> that they're writing about.

2) You can work out what a writer's viewpoint might be by looking for clues in the <u>language</u>, <u>tone</u>, <u>style</u> and <u>content</u> of a text. For example:

> *I urge you to visit this truly unique and hidden valley — you must see such beautiful scenery at least once in your life.*

→

This text's <u>purpose</u> is to <u>persuade</u> its audience to visit a place. The <u>author's viewpoint</u> is their <u>belief</u> that the valley is beautiful and that it should be visited. The writer uses <u>emotive adjectives</u> and an <u>upbeat tone</u> to convey their viewpoint.

Use the writers' Tone to make Inferences about Attitude

PAPER 2

1 6 | Both of these texts are about etiquette. Compare the following:
- the writers' attitudes to etiquette;
- how they get across their arguments.

19th-century etiquette guide

The way you behave when out in society is paramount. It is essential that you show the highest level of social refinement possible. For example, if someone offers you their hand, take it. Always remove your hat when entering a building. Be punctual to all social events to which you are invited.

21st-century newspaper article

Anyone who's ever taken a ride on the London Underground will know that there are some real nuisances out there. All too often, I've seen people refusing to give their seat up to an elderly passenger. I mean, it's just common courtesy, isn't it? Is it really so difficult to just be a little more civil towards other people?

Try to make your observations as perceptive as possible. Examiners will be really impressed if you can pick out subtle differences between the writers' attitudes.

The authors of both sources largely agree that being polite is important. However, there are **subtle differences** in their attitudes. The 19th century writer uses a confident, assured tone, which is created by the use of **imperative verbs** such as "take" and "remove". They also give their advice using the **pronoun** "you", which makes the text sound more like a series of commands than a piece of advice. These things suggest that their ideas about "refinement" are very strict.

Use technical terms to discuss the different methods both writers use to convey their attitudes.

By contrast, the newspaper article has a more relaxed tone. Rather than instructing the reader how to behave, the writer uses rhetorical questions to make the reader think about why people should be "more civil". This is possibly because **the newspaper article is from the 21st century, whereas the etiquette guide was written in the 19th century, when etiquette was considered to be more important.**

This is a useful phrase to use when you're linking the two texts.

Think about the reasons why their attitudes differ — think about when and why they were written.

EXAM TIP ## Comment on how attitudes are conveyed...

To get top marks, you'll need to think about <u>how</u> a writer expresses their views, not just what they say. Even if two writers have the same opinion, one might express it more strongly than the other.

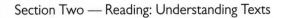

Literature

In paper 1, you'll be given an extract from a piece of literature, and you need to be able to analyse it.

Literature **Entertains** the reader

1) Literature, such as a novel or short story, is written to <u>entertain</u>. It might do this by affecting the reader's <u>emotions</u>, describing the <u>atmosphere</u> of a place, using an intriguing <u>structure</u> or developing the <u>personality</u> of a <u>character</u>.

2) All literature has a <u>narrator</u>. It's most often either a <u>first-person</u> (uses 'I' and 'we') or <u>third-person</u> (uses 'he', 'she' and 'they') narrator.

3) Literature uses lots of <u>descriptive</u> and <u>figurative</u> language (e.g. metaphors, similes, analogy and personification) to capture the reader's <u>imagination</u>.

4) Literature is also <u>structured</u> to interest the reader — texts will often build the <u>tension</u> towards a dramatic climax, or they might use <u>repetition</u> and varied <u>sentence structures</u> to change the <u>pace</u> of a text.

5) <u>Dialogue</u> is also often used to move the plot along and give insight into the <u>thoughts</u> and <u>feelings</u> of different characters.

See section 3 for more on all these language and structural features.

Look Closely at the **Language** used in a text

PAPER 1

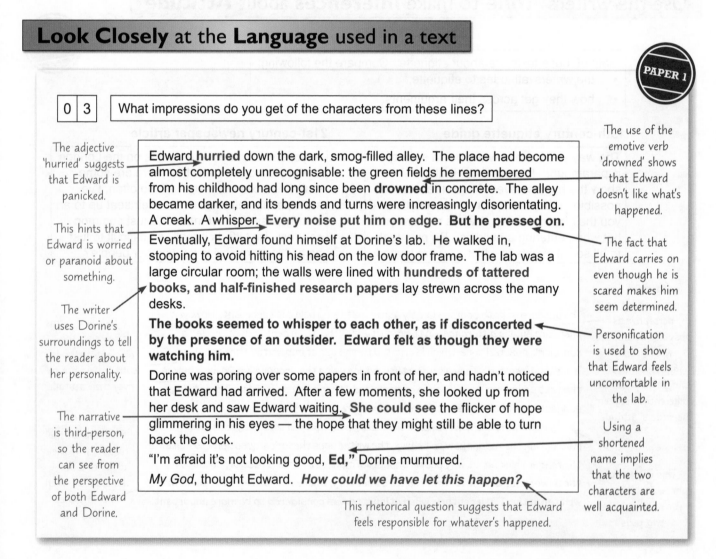

| 0 | 3 | What impressions do you get of the characters from these lines? |

The adjective 'hurried' suggests that Edward is panicked.

This hints that Edward is worried or paranoid about something.

The writer uses Dorine's surroundings to tell the reader about her personality.

The narrative is third-person, so the reader can see from the perspective of both Edward and Dorine.

Edward **hurried** down the dark, smog-filled alley. The place had become almost completely unrecognisable: the green fields he remembered from his childhood had long since been **drowned** in concrete. The alley became darker, and its bends and turns were increasingly disorientating. A creak. A whisper. **Every noise put him on edge. But he pressed on.**

Eventually, Edward found himself at Dorine's lab. He walked in, stooping to avoid hitting his head on the low door frame. The lab was a large circular room; the walls were lined with **hundreds of tattered books, and half-finished research papers** lay strewn across the many desks.

The books seemed to whisper to each other, as if disconcerted by the presence of an outsider. Edward felt as though they were watching him.

Dorine was poring over some papers in front of her, and hadn't noticed that Edward had arrived. After a few moments, she looked up from her desk and saw Edward waiting. **She could see** the flicker of hope glimmering in his eyes — the hope that they might still be able to turn back the clock.

"I'm afraid it's not looking good, **Ed,**" Dorine murmured.

My God, thought Edward. ***How could we have let this happen?***

The use of the emotive verb 'drowned' shows that Edward doesn't like what's happened.

The fact that Edward carries on even though he is scared makes him seem determined.

Personification is used to show that Edward feels uncomfortable in the lab.

Using a shortened name implies that the two characters are well acquainted.

This rhetorical question suggests that Edward feels responsible for whatever's happened.

REVISION TASK

You need to practise analysing extracts from literature...

You'll <u>always</u> have to write about literature, so make sure you know your stuff. Choose a passage from a novel or short story, look at the features it contains and make notes on the effect they have.

Literary Non-Fiction

Now it's time for literary non-fiction — literary writing that's based on fact. You'll see this in paper 2.

Literary non-fiction is **Entertaining** but **Factual**

1) Literary non-fiction texts use <u>literary styles</u> and <u>techniques</u>, but they are based on <u>facts</u> or <u>real events</u>.

2) Non-fiction texts such as <u>biographies</u>, <u>autobiographies</u>, and <u>travel writing</u> will often be written in a similar style to literary fiction.

3) They are written to <u>inform</u> the reader about something, but the writer uses a literary style to make it <u>entertaining</u> too. For example, they might use <u>descriptive</u> language and <u>dialogue</u> to make the information more <u>interesting</u> to the reader.

Have a look back at the previous page to remind yourself about literary style.

4) Literary non-fiction is almost always written in the <u>first person</u>, which adds a sense of <u>personality</u> to the text, helping to <u>engage</u> the reader.

5) Since you're only hearing <u>one person's</u> side of things, watch out for <u>bias</u> in literary non-fiction.

Literary non-fiction tries to **Engage** the **Reader**

PAPER 2

| 1 | 4 | | What do you think and feel about the writer's views on the city of Paris? |

Imagery is used to convey the writer's admiration for the city.

The writer's description of their personal feelings helps the reader to engage with the text and understand the writer's views about Paris.

Dearest reader — **I wish today to impart to you some recollections of my summer spent in Paris,** a city which over time has played host to a multitude of great thinkers and artists. A hundred years may have passed since the French Revolution, but **Paris remains a shining beacon of revolutionary spirit.**

The city of Paris has some **spectacular** specimens of architecture. One bright evening, I took a particularly enjoyable stroll down the Champs-Élysées, and was quite amazed by the **stunning** curvature of its Arc de Triomphe. **The arch incited within me the strongest feelings of awe and wonderment; it is truly a structure built to inspire.**

Paris has been ever-popular with the gentleman traveller, but this year the city captures one's imagination more than ever before, as it hosts the annual 'World's Fair'. There I saw many wonderful artefacts, including a magnificent replica of the Bastille, the famous site of the rebellion which began France's Revolution. The replica was incredibly lifelike, from the gloomy outer stonework to the banquet hall within.

Although the fortress was a thrilling diversion, it was far from the real star of the fair — that honour belonged to the newly-erected 'Eiffel Tower', said to be the largest building on Earth. The new tower amazed fair-goers with its enormous metallic form (although some were not altogether thrilled by its brash modernity). Whether one marvels at this remarkable feat of engineering, or recoils from its audacious magnitude, the new tower is assuredly a sight to behold.

This text uses a story-telling style and a first-person narrator to add personality — the writer is trying to engage and entertain the reader.

The text uses lots of emotive adjectives to clearly show the writer's positive attitude towards Paris. Purely informative non-fiction wouldn't use adjectives like these.

This sentence creates suspense by not revealing what the 'real star' is right away — the writer is essentially telling a story, so they try to create some tension for the reader.

Literary non-fiction is not as complicated as it might sound...

Don't let the phrase "literary non-fiction" worry you — it's just a category that describes any text that is factual, but is written in an entertaining way. Have a read of the texts on pages 73 and 77, for example.

19th-Century Texts

In paper 2, you'll always be given a 19th-century non-fiction text. Here's some information about the period.

19th-century Writing is often quite Formal

1) 19th-century texts can sound a bit <u>different</u> to more modern texts, but you should still be able to <u>understand</u> what's going on.

2) A lot of the texts will use a more <u>formal register</u> (see p.33) than modern writing, even if the <u>audience</u> is quite <u>familiar</u> (see next page for an example of this).

3) The sentences may be <u>quite long</u> and the <u>word order</u> can sometimes be different to modern texts. Try not to worry about this — just <u>re-read</u> any sentences you can't make sense of at first. Here are a couple of examples:

Then, Albert being gone and we two left alone, Edward enquired as to whether I might accompany him on a stroll in the garden.		This sentence is written using a <u>formal</u> register, e.g. it uses 'enquired' instead of 'asked'. It might seem a bit <u>confusingly phrased</u> too, but 'Albert being gone and we two left alone' is just <u>another way</u> of saying 'Albert had gone and the two of us were left alone.'

I believe it necessary to abandon this foul enterprise.		Sometimes it can seem as if a word has been <u>missed out</u> — modern writers would probably put 'is' after 'it' in this sentence.

19th-century Society was Different to today

1) Knowing about 19th-century <u>society</u> will help you to <u>understand</u> the text better in the exam.

2) It will also help you to compare the <u>attitudes</u> of writers from different <u>time periods</u>, which you need to do in paper 2.

Social Class

- Early 19th-century society was <u>divided</u> between the rich <u>upper classes</u> (who owned the land) and the poorer <u>working classes</u>.

- Throughout the 19th century, the <u>Industrial Revolution</u> was creating opportunities for more people to make more <u>money</u>.

- This meant that the <u>middle classes</u> grew in <u>number</u> and <u>influence</u> throughout the century.

Education

- In the <u>early</u> 19th century, <u>few</u> children went to school. Children from poor families often <u>worked</u> to help support their families instead.

- In the <u>late</u> 19th century, <u>education reforms</u> made school <u>compulsory</u> for all young children.

- <u>Rich</u> families often sent their children to <u>boarding school</u>, or hired a <u>governess</u> to live with the family and teach the children at <u>home</u>.

Women

- After they got married, most women were expected to be in charge of looking after the <u>home</u> and <u>children</u>.

- Women didn't have as many <u>rights</u> as men — they couldn't <u>vote</u> in elections and they often didn't <u>control</u> their own money and property.

Religion

- Most <u>middle- and upper-class</u> people attended <u>church</u> regularly.

- However, <u>science</u> was starting to challenge some religious ideas, e.g. Darwin's theory of <u>evolution</u> questioned the Bible's account of <u>creation</u>.

19th-Century Texts

Have a look at this piece of 19th-century Writing

This is a letter written to Princess (later Queen) Victoria of the United Kingdom by her uncle, King Leopold I of Belgium. In it, Leopold describes his new wife, Louise Marie.

The tone is affectionate but the register is formal — this is common in 19th-century letters.

Being 'virtuous' was an important quality in 19th-century society — it means having strong morals.

This shows the 19th-century viewpoint of what was valued in upper class women.

You might come across a tricky phrase or sentence. Use the context and the rest of the sentence to work out what's going on. Here, Leopold suggests that Louise Marie doesn't try very hard at playing the harp.

19th-century texts often phrase things differently — here, a modern writer might have said "I should end this letter here."

Laeken, 31st August 1832.

MY DEAREST LOVE,—You told me you wished to have a description of your new Aunt. I therefore shall both mentally and physically describe her to you.

She is extremely gentle and amiable, her actions are always guided by principles. She is at all times ready and disposed to sacrifice her comfort and inclinations to see others happy. She values goodness, merit, and **virtue** much more than beauty, riches, and amusements. With all this she is highly informed and very clever; **she speaks and writes English, German and Italian**; she speaks English very well indeed. In short, my dear Love, you see that I may well recommend her as **an example for all young ladies**, being Princesses or not.

Now to her appearance. She is about Feodore's* height, her hair very fair, light blue eyes, of a very gentle, intelligent and kind expression. A Bourbon** nose and small mouth. The figure is much like Feodore's but rather less stout. **She rides very well,** which she proved to my great alarm the other day, by keeping her seat though a horse of mine ran away with her full speed for at least half a mile. **What she does particularly well is dancing.** Music unfortunately she is not very fond of, though she plays on **the harp; I believe there is some idleness in the case.** There exists already great confidence and affection between us; she is desirous of doing everything that can contribute to my happiness, and I study whatever can make her happy and contented.

You will see by these descriptions that though my good little wife is not the tallest Queen, **she is a very great prize which I highly value and cherish**...

Now it is time I should finish my letter. Say everything that is kind to good Lehzen***, and believe me ever, **my dearest Love**, your faithful Friend and Uncle,

LEOPOLD R.

Upper class women were educated in European languages in the 19th century.

Upper class women were considered to be accomplished by their ability in things like riding, dancing, playing music and speaking languages.

Women were often seen as belonging to their husbands.

Superlatives (e.g. 'kindest', 'most gracious') are common in 19th-century writing.

Glossary

* Feodore — Victoria's half-sister, Princess Feodora

** Bourbon — the Bourbons were the French royal family

*** Lehzen — Princess Victoria's governess, Louise Lehzen

You will definitely have to analyse a 19th-century text in paper 2...

It's important to make sure you're comfortable reading and understanding 19th-century texts. These pages might look more like History than English, but they'll help you to improve some of your answers in paper 2.

Worked Answer

Here's a sample question with a worked answer for you to have a look at. Watch and learn...

---

1 6 Read the following extracts.

> **19th-Century Diary**
> Dear Diary —
>   I've had quite a day today! Daddy and I took a trip to see the new steam train, which was being exhibited in James Square. It was fascinating — a clanking, grinding steel colossus, shiny as a new penny, with a great puff of steam that emerged from its funnel and curled into the summer sky. I've never seen the like — and to think, Daddy says one day they may be able to carry people from one end of the country to the other! I for one cannot wait.

> **21st-Century Speech**
> Residents of Station Crescent! I know that you, like me, are plagued day-in, day-out with the sounds, smells and sights of the railway. Like me, many of you moved here at a time when three or four trains a day passed by, barely disturbing us at all. And like me, you've seen our area systematically invaded by a non-stop army of trains, impacting our quality of life — not to mention the price of our homes. The time has come to take a stand against the relentless growth of the railways.

Both of these texts are about rail transport.

Compare the following:

- the writers' attitudes towards rail transport;
- how they get across their points of view.

You must use the text to support your comments and make it clear which text you are referring to.

---

figurative language — "shiny as a new penny" in diary, army metaphor in speech

rhetorical devices in speech — aims to persuade. Diary is more descriptive e.g. "curled" bit.

exclamation mark for excitement in diary but for emotive effect in speech

diary wants more trains, speech wants fewer trains

> You <u>don't</u> need to make a <u>detailed plan</u> for this type of question, but <u>quickly</u> jotting down your <u>ideas</u> (like this) can be helpful.

This is a great opening sentence. It makes a <u>clear point</u> that is focused on the <u>question</u>.

Use <u>linking words and phrases</u> to show that you're making a <u>comparison</u>.

<u>The writers of both texts use figurative language to convey their attitudes to rail transport.</u> In the 19th-century diary, the train is "shiny as a new penny". <u>This simile suggests that</u> the writer feels the train is exciting because it's so new. <u>In contrast,</u> the figurative language in the 21st-century speech shows the writer's frustration with trains. He uses a metaphor to compare them to a "non-stop army", which makes them seem like a relentless and aggressive nuisance.

This answer <u>identifies</u> a language technique and then explains its <u>effect</u>.

To make this into a top level paragraph, you could mention <u>why</u> they might have these different attitudes by referring to the <u>contexts</u> of the sources.

Section Two — Reading: Understanding Texts

Worked Answer

It's good to think about how the writer has conveyed their attitude through structure, as well as through language.

The attitudes in the speech are conveyed using rhetorical devices. The writer <u>repeats</u> the phrase "like me" to get the audience on side. The writer also uses direct address, such as "Residents of Station Crescent", to suggest that the audience are a united team, who are able to work together to change things. In the diary <u>the attitudes are conveyed using</u> descriptive language, such as <u>"a great puff of steam</u> <u>that emerged from its funnel and curled into the</u> <u>summer sky"</u>. This shows how impressed the writer is by the new trains, feeling they are almost magical.

Phrases like this keep your answer <u>focused</u> on the second bullet point in the question — <u>how</u> the writers get their point of view across...

This quote does <u>support</u> the point, but it would be better to make it much <u>shorter</u> and then explain its effect more <u>specifically</u>.

Both of the writers use exclamation marks to make their attitudes clear. In the diary, they are used by the writer to emphasise their <u>excited attitude</u> to the steam train. On the other hand, in the speech, the writer uses an exclamation mark to show his dedication to the cause and to persuade the audience to agree that <u>the trains are a problem</u>.

...and phrases like these focus on the <u>first</u> bullet point (<u>what</u> the attitudes are and how they're <u>different</u>).

The examiner will want to see that you can analyse the effect of individual words and <u>phrases</u>.

The 19th-century writer hopes that there will be more trains. They "cannot wait" for the trains to be able to carry people from one end of the country to the other, and <u>the phrase "I for one"</u> implies that the author believes other people will feel the same. In the speech, the attitude is very different. This writer wants there to be fewer trains, because there used to be "three or four" and they use <u>the phrase "relentless</u> <u>growth"</u> to suggest to the audience that further expansion poses a real danger to the community.

Each <u>paragraph</u> in this answer makes a <u>new comparison</u> between the writers' attitudes. This shows a <u>clear understanding</u> of the differences.

- This is a good answer. It clearly compares the writers' attitudes (which covers the first bullet point) and it also discusses the writers' methods (which covers the second bullet point).

- To get the very top marks, this answer could be improved by:

  - using the different contexts of the sources to comment on why the attitudes might be different.

  - pointing out more subtle differences in the attitudes, e.g. the writer in the 19th-century diary is writing about seeing one train on one particular day, whereas the writer in the 21st-century speech is writing about living alongside multiple trains every day.

  - making sure that all the quotations are really precise.

Exam-Style Questions

Now that you've seen an example answer, have a go at these exam-style questions for yourself.

Q1   Read the following extracts.

19th-Century Letter
Dear Miss Tinsham,
I read with concern your recent article on the new wave of art reaching British shores. With all due respect, I see it as nothing short of an abomination. It is created with a flagrant disregard for the conventions and traditions of classical art. These 'artists' seem not to have learnt from their predecessors, but instead insist on violating their canvasses with an assault of colour, which to view, in perfect honesty, is simply excruciating.

21st-Century Newspaper Article
The London art scene has rarely been so exciting. We are seeing a real influx of artists who aren't afraid to throw off the iron shackles of 'traditional art' and champion self-expression. They're rule breakers, not intimidated by the giants of the past. They're revolutionaries, constantly looking forward, never back. Only by pushing the boundaries of modern art are we going to see any progression in the medium. When art conforms, it stagnates, and these new experimenters understand that.

Both of these texts are about art.

Compare the following:

- the writers' attitudes towards art;
- how they get across their points of view.

You must use the text to support your comments and make it clear which text you are referring to.

Q2   Read the following extract from a novel.

> Annie went from room to room, shaking her head at the disarray. The house looked as if it had been burgled. In the living room, a bookcase had been thrown onto the floor, and paperbacks were scattered chaotically across the carpet. In the kitchen, the floor was a treacherous landscape of smashed crockery and broken glass.
> Annie frowned and headed cautiously up the stairs, following the crashing sounds into the master bedroom. Lucas stood with his back to her. His hair was a frantic mess, his movements manic as he pulled every item of clothing out of his wardrobe and launched them behind him. He was muttering frenetically under his breath.
> "Lucas," Annie said calmly. He span around, surprised by her presence. His wide eyes were wild, beads of sweat had appeared on his forehead and his cheeks were red.
> "I can't find it," he said. "I've looked everywhere. It's lost. They'll kill me."
> "Don't be ridiculous. They're not going to kick you out just because you've lost your key to the clubhouse," said Annie, her arms folded.
> "What would you know about it?" said Lucas, his eyes flashing in annoyance. "They're obsessed with not letting any outsiders in. If they find out I've lost it... I'm doomed. Finished. Condemned."

"The writer is successful in bringing Annie and Lucas alive for the reader. You feel as if you can identify with both characters." How far do you agree with this view?

You should write about:

- your own impressions of Annie and Lucas;
- how the writer has created these impressions.

You must refer to the text to support your answer.

Revision Summary

It's time for another Revision Summary. If you know your stuff, it will be very quick to complete.

- Try these questions and <u>tick off each one</u> when you <u>get it right</u>.
- When you've done <u>all the questions</u> under a heading and are <u>completely happy</u> with it, tick it off.

Thinking About the Information, Ideas, Audience and Purpose (p.12-15) ☑

1) What is the difference between explicit and implicit information?
2) When summarising information, should you use examples from the texts?
3) Name three things you can look at to work out who a text's audience is.
4) What audience is this Complete Revision and Practice book aimed at?
5) List four common purposes of a piece of writing.

Different Types of Text (p.16-19) ☑

6) Give two examples of an informative text.
7) Can an informative text be biased? How?
8) Which of these techniques might a writer use to make a text entertaining?
   a) an engaging opening
   b) descriptive language
   c) lots of facts
   d) different sentence lengths
9) Write down three rhetorical techniques that might be used to argue or persuade.
10) How is the tone of writing that advises usually different from writing that argues or persuades?
11) True or false? *Texts that advise are always written in a formal register.*

The Writer's Viewpoint in Different Texts (p.23-27) ☑

12) What is the difference between the writer's viewpoint and the writer's purpose?
13) Give three things you could look at in a text to work out what the writer's viewpoint is.
14) What is the main purpose of literature?
15) What is literary non-fiction?
16) Write down whether the following texts are literature or literary non-fiction.
   a) the autobiography of a retired professional cricketer
   b) a short story about a trip to the seaside
   c) a piece of travel writing about Rome
   d) an opinion piece in a broadsheet newspaper
17) Is the register of a 19th-century text likely to be formal or informal?
18) Write down whether the following statements are true or false.
   a) Most middle- and upper-class people went to church in the 19th century.
   b) After they got married, most 19th-century women were expected to go out to work.
   c) Poor children were often sent away to boarding schools in the 19th century.
   d) Early 19th-century society was divided into the upper classes and working classes.
   e) Women didn't have as many rights as men in the 19th century.

Tone

Tone can sometimes be difficult to describe, but it comes through in the text's language.

Tone is the **General Feeling** created by the text

1) A writer's tone is the <u>feeling</u> the words are written with, which creates a particular <u>mood</u> and shows what the writer's <u>attitude</u> is. For example, the tone of a text might be:

- happy or sad
- serious or funny
- sombre or light-hearted
- emotional and passionate or cool and logical

2) The main way to identify a text's tone is by looking at the <u>language</u>. For example, if a writer has used <u>informal</u> language, the tone might be quite <u>personal</u> or <u>familiar</u>, but <u>formal</u> language would suggest a more <u>serious</u> or <u>distant</u> tone.

Think of a writer's tone as being like someone's tone of voice when they're talking.

3) <u>Punctuation</u> can also give you a clue about tone. For example, if there are lots of exclamation marks, that might suggest that the tone is very <u>emotional</u> or <u>passionate</u>.

4) Tone can reflect the <u>purpose</u> of a text (e.g. informative texts usually have a serious tone) or the <u>audience</u> (e.g. a playful tone might suggest a younger audience).

Look closely at **Language** to **Work Out** a text's **Tone**

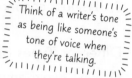

PAPER 1

| 0 | 5 | "In this passage, the writer makes the reader feel uneasy." |

To what extent do you agree with this view?

The adjectives used help to create the foreboding tone.

Phillipa stood on the cold, dark street, peering up at the abandoned hotel. Large wooden boards stood impassively across most of the window frames, sentries to the stillness and silence within, guarding the eerie presence of the dilapidated building.

Despite her misgivings, she pushed gently on the front door, and it crept open with an arthritic creak. As she tiptoed over the threshold, small clouds of dust wheezed out of the carpet where she put her feet.

The sinister tone is gripping for the reader, which keeps the text entertaining.

Don't forget to mention how much you agree or disagree with the statement.

Remember to use technical terms wherever possible.

I **strongly agree** with this view. The heavily foreboding tone, created by **adjectives** such as "abandoned", "eerie" and "dilapidated", and **reinforced by** the **personification** of the "wooden boards" as silent "sentries", gives the passage a tense atmosphere. The **reader shares** in the fear and anxiety of the character, as you feel that something shocking could happen at any moment. The imagery of something cold and emotionless watching over the character **makes you feel** her vulnerability and fear for what might happen next.

Mention the combined effect of different features of the text.

You need to make sure you refer back to the statement for questions like this.

Some tones are easier to spot than others...

Sometimes, the tone of a text will be obvious. But watch out for texts that are written with an ironic or sarcastic tone — the words might not mean exactly what they seem to at first (take a look at pages 42-43).

Style and Register

Every text you come across will be written in a particular style, using a particular register...

Style is How the text is Written

1) A text's <u>style</u> is the overall way in which it's written, which includes <u>language choices</u>, <u>sentence forms</u> and <u>structure</u>.

2) There are lots of <u>different styles</u> you might encounter. E.g. <u>cinematic</u>, where the text is written as if the reader is watching a film, or <u>journalistic</u> which is a balanced way of writing reported news.

3) <u>Register</u> is the specific language (choice of words) used to match the writing to the <u>social situation</u> that it's for. Different situations require <u>different</u> registers, for example:

> If you wrote a letter to your <u>local MP</u> to ask them to stop the closure of a local leisure centre, you might use a <u>formal register</u> (e.g. 'the closure will have a detrimental effect'). This is because the audience is an <u>authority figure</u> that you <u>don't know</u>.

> If you wrote a letter to your <u>friend</u> to tell them about the leisure centre closure, you might use an <u>informal register</u> (e.g. 'it'll be rubbish when it shuts'). This is because the audience is someone you're <u>familiar</u> and <u>friendly</u> with.

Register can be thought of as a part of style.

4) Look out for how writers <u>adapt</u> their style and register to suit the <u>purpose</u> and the <u>audience</u> they are writing for.

Write about Style and Register when Analysing Language

PAPER 2

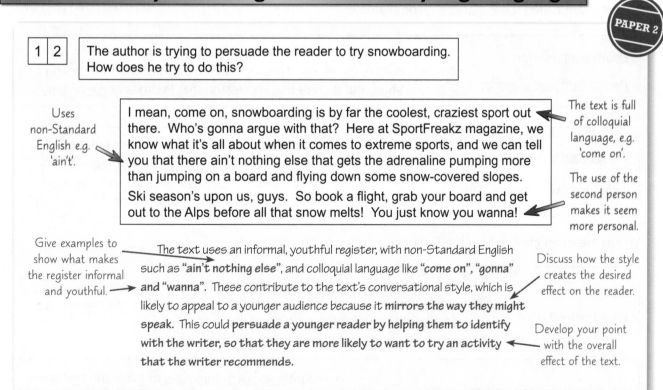

| 1 | 2 | The author is trying to persuade the reader to try snowboarding. How does he try to do this? |

Uses non-Standard English e.g. 'ain't'.

> I mean, come on, snowboarding is by far the coolest, craziest sport out there. Who's gonna argue with that? Here at SportFreakz magazine, we know what it's all about when it comes to extreme sports, and we can tell you that there ain't nothing else that gets the adrenaline pumping more than jumping on a board and flying down some snow-covered slopes.
>
> Ski season's upon us, guys. So book a flight, grab your board and get out to the Alps before all that snow melts! You just know you wanna!

The text is full of colloquial language, e.g. 'come on'.

The use of the second person makes it seem more personal.

Give examples to show what makes the register informal and youthful.

The text uses an informal, youthful register, with non-Standard English such as **"ain't nothing else"**, and colloquial language like **"come on", "gonna" and "wanna"**. These contribute to the text's conversational style, which is likely to appeal to a younger audience because it **mirrors the way they might speak**. This could **persuade a younger reader by helping them to identify with the writer, so that they are more likely to want to try an activity that the writer recommends.**

Discuss how the style creates the desired effect on the reader.

Develop your point with the overall effect of the text.

You need to comment on how style and register are created...

Style has to do with language and vocabulary, structure, tone... so think about how the style is built up from all these different features. You also need to think about the text's register and how it's been achieved.

Words and Phrases

Writers choose their words very carefully to produce a desired effect, and you need to comment on this.

Writers use a range of Word Types

It's important to be able to identify the <u>types</u> of words that a writer is using.
Have a look at the <u>definitions</u> below to remind you:

> <u>Nouns</u> are naming words — they might refer to a person, place, thing or idea, e.g. sister, pen, art.
>
> A <u>pronoun</u> is a word that replaces a noun, e.g. he, she, it, them.
>
> <u>Possessive pronouns</u> are pronouns that show ownership, e.g. his, hers, ours, theirs.
>
> <u>Verbs</u> are action words, e.g. think, run, swim, shout.
>
> <u>Adjectives</u> describe a noun or pronoun, e.g. happy, clever, interesting.
>
> <u>Adverbs</u> give extra information about verbs, e.g. quickly, loudly, accidentally.

Words and Phrases can be used to achieve Different Effects

1) For the <u>reading</u> questions (section A on both papers), you need to pay close attention to the reasons <u>why</u> a writer has used particular <u>words</u> or <u>phrases</u>.

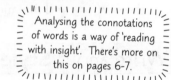
Analysing the connotations of words is a way of 'reading with insight'. There's more on this on pages 6-7.

2) Words can have subtle <u>implications</u> beyond their obvious meaning — these are called '<u>connotations</u>'. For example:

Pedro <u>shut</u> the door. *Pedro <u>slammed</u> the door.*	When the verb 'shut' is used, it <u>doesn't</u> imply anything about Pedro's <u>emotions</u>. The verb 'slammed' has a similar meaning to 'shut', but it gives the impression that Pedro is <u>angry</u> or <u>tense</u>.
I <u>sniggered</u> when I saw Peter's costume. *I <u>chuckled</u> when I saw Peter's costume.*	The verbs 'sniggered' and 'chuckled' both mean the writer <u>laughed</u>, but 'sniggered' has a slightly <u>nastier</u> connotation — as if the writer is making fun of Peter.

3) Words are often chosen to achieve particular <u>effects</u>. For example:

Determiners are words that help to identify nouns — in this case, they show who the noun belongs to.

<u>my</u> dear reader *<u>your</u> beloved pet*	Phrases that use the <u>possessive determiners</u> 'my', 'your' and 'our' help to establish <u>familiarity</u> between the writer and the reader.
a <u>fundamentally</u> flawed proposition *a <u>totally</u> unbelievable situation*	Some phrases use <u>intensifiers</u> to make the text seem more <u>emotive</u> and <u>powerful</u>. Intensifiers are adverbs like 'very', 'really' or 'extremely' that are used <u>alongside</u> strong adjectives to provide <u>emphasis</u>.

Words and Phrases

Words **Work Together** to create **Cumulative Effects**

1) Writers can use the words from a specific <u>semantic field</u> (the words associated with a particular <u>theme</u> or <u>topic</u>) to convey an idea to the reader. For example:

> *Dessert was simply <u>divine</u>; a <u>cloud-like</u> puff of pastry that was lighter than an <u>angel's wing</u>.*

→ Here, the <u>semantic field</u> of <u>heaven</u> is used to make something sound <u>appealing</u>.

2) Keep an eye out for situations where particular <u>types</u> of words are <u>repeated</u>, e.g. sentences with lots of <u>adjectives</u> or paragraphs with lots of <u>verbs</u>.

3) You could comment on the <u>cumulative effect</u> of particular types of words — show you've thought about how the words in the text <u>work together</u> to create <u>tone</u> or <u>affect</u> the reader in some way, e.g.

> *Adjectives like 'electrifying', 'thrilling', 'tense' and 'intriguing' create a cumulative effect of <u>excitement</u>.*

> *The adverbs 'jovially', 'readily' and 'pleasantly' combine to create an impression of <u>enjoyment</u>.*

Try to pick out **Significant Words** and **Phrases**

PAPER 2

| 1 | 2 | The author is trying to persuade us to choose Bijoux Birthdays. How do they try to do this? |

Adjectives like 'magical', 'beautiful', 'balmy', 'glistening' and 'sumptuous' have a pleasant cumulative effect — they create a calming atmosphere.

Watch out for repeated grammatical constructions — they give the text emphasis.

A PICTURE-PERFECT PICNIC

Bijoux Birthdays invite you to celebrate **your special day** in style. Join us for a **magical** evening of entertainment on the **beautiful** banks of the River Fairer. Let us help you to **relax** in the **balmy** atmosphere of a warm summer's evening, **recline** next to the **glistening** waters and **indulge** in the most **sumptuous** of picnics.

We can tailor your evening to suit you. **We can** provide a refreshing feast for your senses. **We can** transport you to another place and time. Just **sit back** and **let us** do all the work. All you need to do is relax.

We have a large selection of menus for you to choose from, as well as a whole host of different entertainment acts — **maybe** you'd like a string quartet, or **perhaps** you'd be more interested in a circus act? Whatever your tastes, rest assured that we will be able to accommodate you.

Phrases that use possessive determiners establish familiarity with the reader and make the text more persuasive.

The list of three verbs — 'relax', 'recline' and 'indulge' — gives the text a convincing tone and makes the offer sound inviting.

Imperatives like 'sit back' and 'let us' give the text an authoritative tone, whilst the words 'perhaps' and 'maybe' give the impression that the reader has a choice.

Comments like "this is an adjective" aren't quite good enough...

Don't just point out the technical grammar of words and phrases — you need to analyse its effects too. Think about why certain words and phrases have been used and the impression they create.

Warm-Up Questions

Before you answer the exam-style questions on the right, give these ones a go as a handy warm-up.

Warm-Up Questions

1) Is the tone of each of the following sentences sentimental, detached or upbeat?
   a) Investigators have recently confirmed that DNA found at the scene of the burglary matches that of suspect Fergus Maybach.
   b) I had a riot helping out at the birthday party — who would've guessed that kids were the perfect audience for my magic tricks?
   c) As he stared across the bay where they had first met, he remembered vividly the tinkle of her laughter and the floral scent of her hair.

2) Which of the sentences in question 1 is written in a journalistic style?

3) What is the tone of the following text? Explain your answer.

> At this point I was starting to get a tad — how shall I put it? — cheesed off. It's one thing being patient, accepting the fact that things don't always go to plan and that now and then delays just happen. It's quite another to be told, after paying good money for a ticket to Town A, that for no good reason you're taking a little detour through Village B, River C and Swamp D. I was finding it more and more difficult to follow what I had figured was the local way of dealing with difficulties — smiling and pretending to find the grim industrial scenery interesting. It wasn't.

4) Rewrite each of the following sentences so that they are in a formal register.
   a) Sorry, we don't take credit cards!
   b) Check you've got the proper kit to hand before you go any further.

5) Write down the noun, verb and adverb in this sentence: "Bella approached us excitedly."

6) Explain the different connotations of the underlined words in the sentences below.
   "Just go," she <u>whispered</u>.
   "Just go," she <u>spat</u>.

7) a) Is the semantic field of the passage below i) Shakespeare, ii) money or iii) shellfish?
   b) What impression does this create of the narrator?

> I wasn't interested in seeing my sister's school Shakespeare play, but I couldn't afford to miss being at the theatre that night. The owner of DigTech was going to be there watching his daughter, and I was desperate to sell him my latest design idea. I decided to buy myself some extra time by locking him inside the gents toilets with me during the interval. A bit drastic, perhaps, but you have to cash in on this sort of opportunity.

8) What is the cumulative effect of the verbs in this sentence?
   The wind barged across the barren, open moorland and threw itself against the stoic stone walls of the cottage, wrenching the window shutters from their frames.

Exam-Style Questions

Here are a couple of exam-style questions for you to have a go at. Keep in mind the theory you've just been reading about in this section — the writer's use of tone, style, register, and words and phrases.

Q1   Read the following extract from a short story.

> The wind rose suddenly. It was a bitter wind, a stinging wind, a wind that drowned all thoughts in a roaring cacophony of noise and fury. It was a tempest that barged across the barren, open moorland and threw itself against the stoic stone walls of the cottage. We didn't know when there would be an end to its howling or its persistent, unruly attempts to gain entry into our little home.
>
> We fought back the best we knew how. We had already nailed boards against the window shutters to stop them being wrenched open by the gusts; now we rolled up old rags and laid them against the gaps in the door frames to resist the draughts. Still it savaged us.
>
> "It can't get much worse, can it?" I asked Father, raising my voice above the roar of the enemy outside. His eyebrows drew together sternly.
>
> "We're just going to have to sit it out," he said. "We don't have any alternative."

How does the writer show the effect of the weather?

You must refer to the language used in the text to support your answer, using relevant subject terminology.

Q2   Read the following extract from a piece of fiction.

> She raised an eyebrow at him icily. Her mouth was a stern, straight line. It did not twitch.
> "Please," he pleaded, "it was a mistake. It won't happen again."
> Her silence was stone cold. He began to wring his hands fretfully. He could feel the sweat prickling like needles on the back of his neck. The seconds crawled by excruciatingly as he waited for her to say something, anything. He briefly considered speaking, but was too fearful of aggravating her further.
> "Evidently," she said at last, "you can no longer be trusted." The only emotion in her voice was disdain.
> His breath caught painfully in his chest; he knew the worst was coming.
> "I have no use for people I cannot trust," she continued. "You are dismissed. Leave now. Resign your post. Never let me see your face again. Understood?"
> Trembling, he managed a clumsy nod.
> "Good. Now get out."
> He turned and, dragging his feet like a condemned man, left the room.

What impressions does the writer create of the two characters in these lines?

You must refer to the language used in the text to support your answer, using relevant subject terminology.

Metaphors and Similes

Metaphors and similes are both types of imagery — writers use them to help readers imagine things vividly.

Metaphors and Similes are Comparisons

1) Metaphors and similes describe one thing by <u>comparing</u> it to something else.

> <u>Metaphors</u> describe something by saying that it <u>is</u> something else. → *His gaze <u>was</u> a laser beam, shooting straight through me.*

> <u>Similes</u> describe something by saying that it's <u>like</u> something else. They usually use the words <u>as</u> or <u>like</u>. → *Walking through the bog was <u>like</u> wading through treacle.*

2) They help writers to make their <u>descriptions</u> more creative and interesting.

3) Metaphors usually create a <u>more powerful image</u> than similes, because they describe something as if it <u>actually were</u> something else.

4) Metaphors and similes are most commonly used in <u>literature</u> and <u>literary non-fiction</u>.

 See pages 24-25 for more on literature and literary non-fiction.

Comment on the Effect of Metaphors and Similes

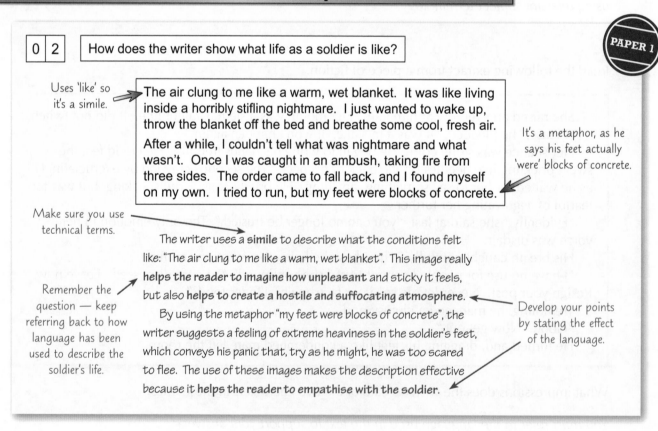

PAPER 1

| 0 | 2 | How does the writer show what life as a soldier is like? |

Uses 'like' so it's a simile.

The air clung to me like a warm, wet blanket. It was like living inside a horribly stifling nightmare. I just wanted to wake up, throw the blanket off the bed and breathe some cool, fresh air.

After a while, I couldn't tell what was nightmare and what wasn't. Once I was caught in an ambush, taking fire from three sides. The order came to fall back, and I found myself on my own. I tried to run, but my feet were blocks of concrete.

It's a metaphor, as he says his feet actually 'were' blocks of concrete.

Make sure you use technical terms.

Remember the question — keep referring back to how language has been used to describe the soldier's life.

The writer uses a **simile** to describe what the conditions felt like: "The air clung to me like a warm, wet blanket". This image really **helps the reader to imagine how unpleasant** and sticky it feels, but also **helps to create a hostile and suffocating atmosphere**.

By using the metaphor "my feet were blocks of concrete", the writer suggests a feeling of extreme heaviness in the soldier's feet, which conveys his panic that, try as he might, he was too scared to flee. The use of these images makes the description effective because it **helps the reader to empathise with the soldier**.

Develop your points by stating the effect of the language.

 REVISION TIP

Learn to spot these two language features...

If you're analysing a text, look out for signs of metaphors or similes. Metaphors say something <u>is</u> something else, whereas a simile says it's <u>like</u> it. Similes often use the words 'as' or 'like'.

Analogy

Writers often use analogies when they're writing to argue or persuade.

Analogies are **Really Fancy Comparisons**

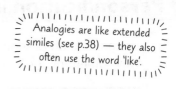

Analogies are like extended similes (see p.38) — they also often use the word 'like'.

1) An analogy <u>compares</u> one idea to another to make it easier to <u>understand</u>.

2) Analogies provide <u>powerful</u> and <u>memorable</u> images. They can be more <u>familiar</u> or more <u>shocking</u> than the original idea, which makes it easier for the reader to <u>grasp the point</u>. For example:

Deforestation is happening at an incredible speed. An area of rainforest equal to twenty football pitches is lost every minute.	By <u>comparing</u> the area to football pitches, the writer makes it easier to <u>visualise</u> the scale of the problem.
Hoping your exams will go OK without opening your books is like hoping to win the lottery without buying a ticket.	By <u>comparing</u> the chances of success to an impossible situation, the writer <u>emphasises</u> how unlikely it is.

3) Analogies are common in <u>non-fiction</u> texts that are trying to <u>argue</u> a point or <u>persuade</u>, as they can help to get the writer's viewpoint across <u>clearly</u> and <u>forcefully</u>.

Think about **Why** the writer has used an **Analogy**

PAPER 2

1 2 The author is trying to persuade the reader to reduce their emissions. How does she try to do this?

> It's easy to throw facts and figures around, but very few people realise we are releasing almost 30 billion tonnes of greenhouse gases into the atmosphere every year. That's the equivalent of around 150 million blue whales.
>
> By pumping these gases into the air, we are choking our planet. This is like starting a fire in your bedroom and slowly letting the room fill with thick, black smoke until you can't breathe.

Uses 'like', so this is another analogy.

The word 'equivalent' shows that this is a comparison.

It's good to make your point straight away. → **The writer uses analogies to help persuade the reader.** By comparing the amount of greenhouse gases released annually to "150 million blue whales", the writer helps the reader to understand and visualise the sheer volume of gas being produced. If they can visualise the problem, readers are more likely to be shocked and therefore share the writer's concerns.

It's great to embed quotes into your writing like this. → The analogy which compares polluting the atmosphere to filling your bedroom with **"thick, black smoke"** makes the threat of climate change seem like a more personal danger to the reader. This might **scare the reader** and help to persuade them to act on climate change.

Always mention the effect that language has on the reader.

Don't worry if you haven't heard of analogies before...

Writers use analogies to make their points clearer and easier to understand. They can also make a piece of writing more interesting — think about how you could use them in the writing section of your exams.

Personification

Personification is another technique that you could comment on in questions about language.

Personification is describing a Thing as a Person

1) Personification describes something as if it's a <u>person</u>. This could be in the way something <u>looks</u>, <u>moves</u>, <u>sounds</u> or some other aspect of it. For example:

Describing an object as if it were alive

The desk groaned under the weight of the books.

Describing an abstract idea as if it were alive

Fear stalked the children with every step they took.

Describing an animal as if it were a person

The cunning fox smiled with a self-satisfied grin.

2) Personification makes a description <u>more vivid</u> (so it '<u>comes to life</u>' for the reader).

3) It can also help to give a sense of the <u>viewpoint</u> or <u>attitude</u> of the <u>writer</u> or <u>character</u>:

Try to think of other ways you could use personification in your own writing.

Military helicopters prowled the city, their menacing mechanical voices threatening to stamp out the smallest sign of activity. ⟹ This shows that the writer feels that the helicopters are an <u>intimidating</u> presence.

Think about How personification Improves a Description

PAPER 1

| 0 | 4 | How does the writer make these lines calm and positive? |

The forest has been given human qualities.

To Catrin's mind, no pastime could better complement a summer's day than a stroll through the woodlands behind her uncle's house.

As soon as she arrived, before she'd even unpacked, she would feel the forest calling to her. It was never long before she wandered into the cool embrace of the sunlight-dappled shade. The trees would smile as she meandered along the paths, and the friendly chatter of wildlife was always the very best company.

The shade has been personified as it embraces the girl.

This is a paraphrase — mentioning something from the text without a direct quote.

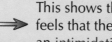
The writer uses personification to create a calm, positive atmosphere in the story. The **smiling trees** and the **"friendly chatter of wildlife"** present parts of the forest as if they were friends of Catrin, which shows that she feels relaxed and at home around them. This is reinforced further by how she is embraced by the "sunlight-dappled shade". By presenting Catrin and the woods as old friends, the writer **keeps the reader feeling calm and positive about what is happening to Catrin as the story progresses.**

Examiners love short embedded quotes like this one.

This is good — it explains the effect of the language.

Link your points back to the question, and mention how the text affects the reader.

REVISION TASK

Try writing some examples of personification...

Coming up with some of your own examples of personification can help you to spot them in a text you're analysing. Have a go at describing a storm, a house and a river using personification.

Alliteration and Onomatopoeia

As well as learning about what alliteration and onomatopoeia are, make sure you can spell them.

Alliteration and Onomatopoeia are about how words Sound

1) Alliteration and onomatopoeia use the <u>sounds</u> of words to create an <u>effect</u>:

<u>Alliteration</u> is when words that are close together begin with the <u>same sound</u>.

PM's panic!   *Close call for kids*

<u>Onomatopoeic</u> words <u>sound like</u> the noises they describe.

thud   squish   smash   crackle   hiss

2) <u>Alliteration</u> helps a writer to grab a reader's <u>attention</u>.

3) It's often used for <u>emphasis</u> and to make key points more <u>memorable</u>.

4) <u>Onomatopoeia</u> makes descriptions more <u>powerful</u> — it appeals to the reader's sense of <u>hearing</u>, which helps them <u>imagine</u> what the writer is describing.

Alliteration and onomatopoeia Keep Readers Interested

PAPER 2

| 1 | 2 | The author is trying to persuade the reader to buy Milkshake Magic. How does he try to do this?

MAKE MILKSHAKE MAGIC!

Just add our Milkshake Magic to a glass of milk, and listen to the powder fizz and crackle into a delicious drink that you'll be slurping up in no time!

The alliteration of 'Milkshake Magic' is repeated for even more emphasis.

'fizz', 'crackle' and 'slurping' are all onomatopoeic.

The writer has used language to interest the target audience of **young children**. The title "Make Milkshake Magic" **uses alliteration to emphasise the idea that the product is "Magic".** This might **persuade the reader to buy it because it implies that the product is something special and unusual.**
The onomatopoeic words "fizz" and "crackle" **create a strong impression of how the drink sounds and make the product seem more exciting.** This is especially likely to gain the interest of younger readers, as it is a lively and fun description of how the product works. **It would help children to imagine themselves using the product,** and therefore make them more likely to buy it.

Show that you realise who the writing is aimed at.

Stay focused on 'how' the language persuades the reader.

Explain why the writer has chosen to use the technique.

Develop the point further if you can.

Think about using these techniques in your own writing...

You need to be able to write about the effects of alliteration and onomatopoeia in the reading sections of both papers, but you could also consider using them in the fiction and non-fiction writing sections.

Irony

Irony can be important for the tone of a piece of writing, so make sure you're comfortable commenting on it.

Irony is **Saying** the **Opposite** of what you **Mean**

1) Irony is when the <u>literal meaning</u> of a piece of writing is the exact <u>opposite</u> of its <u>intended meaning</u>.

2) The reader can tell the writer is being ironic from the <u>context</u> of the writing.

3) Writers often use irony to express their viewpoint, but it helps to make what they're saying more <u>humorous</u> or <u>light-hearted</u>.

> *It was pouring down with rain — perfect weather for a barbecue.* $\longrightarrow$ The <u>context</u> (the rainy weather) shows that the writer actually means that it was <u>terrible</u> weather for a barbecue.

Irony can sometimes be a **Little Tricky** to **Spot**

 PAPER 1

0 5 "In this passage, the writer makes the character's feelings really clear. It feels as if you really get to know her."

To what extent do you agree with this view?

> Clara sat on her lounger at the edge of the pool, thinking of all the poor souls still trapped in the office. She'd been asked to travel to Spain for work. Stay hunched over her cramped, stuffy desk in London or work in this paradise? A very difficult decision indeed.
>
> As the sun rose higher in the sky and the temperature crept up, she thought of dreary, cloudy London. "It's a tough job," she thought to herself, "but somebody's got to do it."

You can tell she is being ironic because of the context — she describes it as a 'paradise', so it can't have been a 'difficult decision'.

Don't forget to mention how much you agree or disagree with the statement.

I **agree** with the first part of this statement, though Clara's feelings are potentially open to misinterpretation. Her comments about a "difficult decision" and a "tough job" are negative if read literally, **but the context makes it clear that they should be taken ironically.** She clearly prefers being in Spain. Her office in London is "cramped", and the people are "trapped", whereas Spain is a "paradise". The irony emphasises just how happy she is by highlighting this contrast.

Make sure you clearly explain why the language is ironic.

I also **strongly agree** with the second part of the statement. Her ironic tone shows that she isn't too serious, but that she is also perhaps quite unsympathetic. The contrast between her situation and that of the "poor souls" in the London office shows that whilst she is "thinking of all" of them, she is most interested in her own pleasant situation. **As a reader, this makes me unsure as to whether I like her character or not.**

A further personal response is a good way to develop your answer.

 EXAM TIP

To work out if something is ironic, look at the context...

The context usually makes it clear whether something is ironic or serious. So if you don't know whether something is ironic or not, reading the whole paragraph should help you to decide.

Sarcasm

There is a subtle difference between sarcasm and irony — have a look at this page.

Sarcasm is Nastier than Irony

1) Sarcasm is language that has a mocking or scornful tone. It's often intended to insult someone or make fun of them, or to show that the writer is angry or annoyed about something.

2) Sarcastic writing usually uses irony — but the tone is more aggressive and unpleasant.

> *The food took 90 minutes to arrive, which was just brilliant. I can think of no better way to spend a Saturday evening than waiting around for a plate of mediocre mush.*

The writer's used irony and a sarcastic tone to show his frustration and anger — it's meant to insult the restaurant that kept him waiting.

3) Satire is a kind of writing that uses sarcasm to make fun of a particular person or thing — it's often used in journalism and reviews.

Explain How you can tell a comment is Sarcastic

PAPER 2

| 1 | 6 |

Both of these texts are about an economic proposal. Compare the following:
* the writers' attitudes to the proposal;
* how they get across their arguments.

Source A

The Government's new economic proposal lays out an excellent path for our economy. Their plan will put more money where it is needed, which is exactly what this country needs right now.

This shows a clearly positive attitude...

... so this feels like a sincere opinion.

Source B

The Government's really outdone itself with this latest economic plan. A lovely gift to the taxpayers, who will now be under even greater financial strain. All in all, exactly what this country needs right now.

The context is negative...

... so this feels like a sarcastic tone.

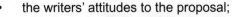

Nice opening — it gets straight to the point.

The writers' opinions differ greatly. Source A looks at the Government's new plan as a positive thing, describing it as **"excellent"**, whereas Source B uses a heavily sarcastic tone to criticise it. The plan is clearly not a "lovely gift to the taxpayers", as they will be under more "financial strain".

Use short quotes within your own sentences.

Use technical terms.

It is interesting that both writers describe the economic proposal as "exactly" what the country "needs", but with different effects. Source A's **tone** is sincere, whereas **the negative context of Source B** makes it clear that the writer is being sarcastic, and believes that the plan is in fact the exact opposite of "what this country needs right now". This method of **ridiculing** the Government's plan may **influence the reader** to agree with the writer's point of view by making the proposal seem so ridiculous that it can't be taken seriously.

Explain how you know that the writer's being sarcastic.

Explain the effect on the reader.

Explain the effect that the use of sarcasm has.

Sarcasm is often used to ridicule someone or something...

Sarcasm can be quite an unpleasant technique to use, but it's also a very effective one. Remember to explain how you know that a piece of writing is sarcastic, and also explain the effect of the sarcasm.

Rhetoric

Rhetorical techniques make language more persuasive. Lots of speeches use rhetoric, for example (see p.78).

There are **Lots** of **Rhetorical Techniques**

Think about how other techniques (e.g. alliteration, sarcasm) could be used as rhetorical devices.

1) <u>Rhetorical questions</u> require no answer — they make readers <u>engage</u> with the text and realise the answer <u>for themselves</u>. This makes the reader feel like they're making up their <u>own mind</u>, when actually the writer is trying to make them think a certain way.

> *Is it right that footballers are paid such vast sums of money?*

2) Writers often use a <u>list of three</u> words or phrases to <u>emphasise</u> the point they're making. They often repeat three adjectives.

> *The cross-country run is <u>painful</u>, <u>pointless</u> and pure <u>evil</u>.*

3) <u>Hyperbole</u> is intentional exaggeration. It's used to make a point very <u>powerfully</u>.

> *We had to wait <u>forever</u> for the food to arrive.*

4) <u>Antithesis</u> is a technique where <u>opposing</u> words or ideas are presented <u>together</u> to show a <u>contrast</u>.

> *Just a <u>small</u> donation from you could have <u>huge</u> consequences for others.*

5) <u>Parenthesis</u> is when an <u>extra</u> clause or phrase is inserted into a complete sentence. Parenthesis can be used in many ways, such as to add <u>extra</u> information or to <u>directly address</u> the reader.

> *This issue, <u>as I'm sure you all agree</u>, is of the highest importance.*

Rhetorical devices **Add Impact** to an **Argument**

PAPER 2

1 2 The author is trying to persuade the reader that students shouldn't be given more homework. How does he try to do this?

Here's some hyperbole.

The writer uses 'we' and 'us' to include the reader.

> This plan to give students across the country more homework is shocking. Can it really be fair to set us even more ridiculous and unnecessary assignments? It's as if they don't think we work every hour God sends already! Join me if you're interested in a better work/life balance. Join me to make our voices heard. Join me in my campaign for less homework!

This is a rhetorical question.

The writer repeats 'join me' three times.

Analysing the effect on the reader develops 'how' the writer has argued their point.

It's good to link your points together wherever possible.

The writer **uses a number of rhetorical devices** to persuade the reader that students should not be given more homework. The rhetorical question about whether it's fair to set more homework assignments is used to engage the reader. When combined with the forceful adjectives "ridiculous" and "unnecessary", this **makes the reader think that it isn't fair**, and therefore agree with the writer's point of view. This is **immediately followed** by the assertion that students are already working "every hour God sends". This hyperbolic statement makes an emphatic point about how hard students work, which generates sympathy from the reader and enhances the argument that more homework would be "**shocking**".

Opening statement is really focused on 'how' the writer argues their point.

Using the writer's words really backs up your analysis of their viewpoint.

There are many other rhetorical techniques...

Remember, there are lots of different types of rhetorical techniques — this page just tells you about some of the most common ones. Make sure you analyse the effect of a rhetorical technique if you spot one.

Bias

If a text is biased, it doesn't give a balanced view — the writer's opinion affects the writing.

Biased writing is **Affected** by the **Writer's Opinions**

1) Biased writers don't usually lie, but they don't give a <u>balanced overview</u> of an argument.

2) Sometimes the writer <u>won't mention</u> something that opposes their viewpoint, or they'll <u>exaggerate</u> something that supports it.

3) Biased writing also often uses <u>generalisations</u> — sweeping statements that aren't necessarily true.

4) Bias isn't always <u>obvious</u>, or even <u>deliberate</u>. Biased writers often <u>seem</u> to be talking in a neutral, factual way — while actually only presenting one point of view.

5) You need to be able to <u>recognise</u> bias, so that you don't mistake opinion for fact.

6) Look out for bias in non-fiction texts like <u>newspaper articles</u> and <u>reviews</u>.

Bias **Weakens** a writer's **Argument**

PAPER 2

| 1 | 6 | Both of these texts are about *Romeo and Juliet*. Compare the following:
• the writers' attitudes to *Romeo and Juliet*;
• how they get across their arguments. |

Biased writers may use hyperbole if they are trying to convince you about something.

They often make opinions sound like facts.

19th-century review

Romeo and Juliet, without the slightest shadow of a doubt, is the very greatest work of literature to have ever been penned in the English language. It truly is the pinnacle of Shakespeare's momentous talent and will never be matched by any playwright to come.

21st-century biography

Romeo and Juliet is one of the most well-known and widely studied works of literature to have ever been penned in the English language. It was among the most popular of Shakespeare's plays during his lifetime, and it is still performed to this day.

Develop your point by writing about the writer's purpose and how successful they are.

Mention the overall difference between the two texts.

The review is written in a very biased way. Hyperbolic statements such as "without the slightest shadow of a doubt" emphasise the writer's strength of feeling, but the statements are unjustified. This bias presents the reader with an **emphatic** argument for how good the play is, but nothing to back it up. **This may convince some readers to watch the play, but others may feel the argument is quite weak.**

Although the biography is also positive about 'Romeo and Juliet', the writer bases their viewpoint on factual statements, describing the play as "well-known" and "widely studied". The writer of the biography is also careful to use phrases like "one of the most" and "among the most", which shows that they are aware that there are other successful and popular plays. **Overall, the biography presents a more balanced viewpoint towards Romeo and Juliet.**

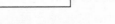 Try to use more interesting vocabulary to get across your exact meaning.

 REVISION TASK

Make sure you know how to spot bias in a text...

Have a go at spotting biased statements in a range of different newspaper articles. Look out for instances where the writer uses exaggeration, makes generalisations or presents opinion as fact.

Descriptive Language

You'll find descriptive language in both literature and literary non-fiction texts.

Descriptive Language makes text Interesting

1) Writers use descriptive <u>techniques</u> and <u>vocabulary</u> so that the reader gets a really clear <u>image</u> in their mind of what the writer's describing. It makes the text more <u>interesting</u>, dramatic and <u>convincing</u>.

2) <u>Descriptive techniques</u> include <u>imagery</u> such as metaphors, similes and personification (see p.38-40).

3) Writers often give <u>descriptions</u> based on their five <u>senses</u> (what they can <u>see</u>, <u>smell</u>, <u>hear</u>, <u>touch</u> or <u>taste</u>).

4) Another sign of descriptive language is when the writer uses lots of <u>adjectives</u> — describing words like 'huge' or 'fiery' that give a specific <u>impression</u> of something.

5) Writers might also use interesting <u>verbs</u>, such as 'saunter' instead of 'walk' to make their descriptions really <u>specific</u>.

> *The sun was setting over the sea.*
> *The view from the beach was incredible.*
>
> → This example relies on the reader to picture <u>for themselves</u> what a nice sunset might look like.
>
> *The salty sea air whooshed around me as the dark-orange sun melted into the horizon, dyeing the cobalt sky a deep crimson.*
>
> → This one uses interesting <u>adjectives</u> and <u>verbs</u> to help the reader to picture and even 'feel' what's going on.

6) Writers can also <u>build up</u> the description of something <u>throughout</u> their work. For example, by writing sentences with <u>contrasting</u> descriptions or descriptions that <u>agree</u> with each other.

Talk about the Effects of Specific Words

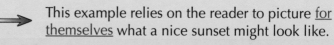

PAPER 1

| 0 | 3 | What impressions do you get about how Deepak feels from these lines? |

Describes the smell to add to the description.

The building is personified to emphasise that it is intimidating.

> Deepak crept slowly towards the tall, dark, brooding building, coming to a standstill in its looming shadow. Smoke billowed from its many chimneys, stinging his eyes and filling his nostrils with an overpowering, acrid smell. He watched the other workers scuttling in through the iron gates. With the tall building glowering down at him, he shuddered, forced his right foot out in front of his left, and began to traipse towards the doors.

Uses a lot of interesting verbs and adjectives.

It's great to talk about the effects of specific words.

The writer uses descriptive language to make it clear that Deepak is feeling very intimidated. The verbs "crept" and "traipse" both carry a negative connotation: they **imply walking very slowly and reluctantly**, as if the character is unwilling to approach the building. His reluctance is also shown in the phrase, "forced his right foot out in front of his left". The verb "forced", **coupled with the extra detail** of exactly how he moved his feet, shows that it is a considerable effort.

Mention if language techniques work together to create an effect.

Be prepared to come across descriptive language in your exams...

Look out for descriptive language in the literature extract in paper 1, and in any literary non-fiction you get in paper 2. Make sure you write about the effect it has, focusing on the specific words and phrases used.

Warm-Up Questions

Use these warm-up questions to test your knowledge of language techniques, then have a go at some of the exam-style questions on the next two pages. Ready, set, write...

Warm-Up Questions

1) What impression is created by this metaphor?
The glassy eye of the lake watched us in silent judgement.

2) Read the texts below. How does the use of an analogy in the second text make it more effective?

> *A running tap wastes around 6 litres of water for every minute it's left running.*

> *A running tap wastes the equivalent of seventeen cups of tea for every minute it's left running.*

3) Write down whether each of the sentences below use personification, alliteration or onomatopoeia. Then explain the effect that the technique creates.
   a) The computer grumbled into life, before smugly informing me that it required six hours of updates.
   b) The buzz and chatter of the students ruined the tranquillity of the scene.
   c) Bag a Bargain at Brigson's — Portsmouth's Premier Pig Farm!

4) Briefly explain the difference between irony and sarcasm.

5) Is the following text sarcastic? Explain your answer using an example from the text.

> Oh yeah, Ivan is a brilliant secretary — I especially appreciate the way he keeps forgetting to bring a pen and steals mine instead. And he's reorganised our files into a brand new system, which only he can understand — that's really made our lives easier.

6) For each sentence below, name the rhetorical technique and then explain its effect.
   a) Far from the sandwich heaven I'd been hoping for, I found myself in sandwich hell.
   b) I urge you, dear readers, to avoid this new restaurant at all costs.
   c) There's nothing worse than rain during an outdoor theatre performance.

7) Explain why the following text is biased. Use evidence from the text to support your answer.

> By far the best hobby for young people is the card game "cribbage". All young people from the ages of eight to eighteen adore playing cribbage.

8) Write a paragraph about the effect of some of the descriptive language in the text below.

> The air smelt of scorched grass. I could feel the blistering sun burning into my skin as I trudged slowly through the prickly, dry vegetation, my heavy load cutting cruel lines into my drooping shoulders. In the distance, the air shimmered in waves with the heat. I felt as if I were underwater, constantly being pulled back by the tidal drag of the temperature, every step an effort, every breath a trial.

Exam-Style Questions

To answer these exam-style questions, you need to draw on all of your knowledge about language techniques — have a quick glance back at pages 38-46 to refresh your memory, then get stuck into this lot.

Q1 Read the following extract from a piece of fiction.

> The landscape was dull steel. The sea was grey, the sky was grey and the mountains in the distance were grey. And we were grey too. Our meagre rations of bread and nameless slop had left us sallow-faced, with dark rings under our eyes. We huddled together nervously, like mice in a cage. A thin layer of snow carpeted the tundra already. It was only September; there would be plenty more snow to come. The wind whipped at our cheeks and we shivered.
>
> The soldiers were smoking by the hut, casting sideways glances at us once in a while, to make sure that we weren't doing anything foolish, like trying to escape. Eventually they trampled on their cigarettes and marched over to us — wolves in military uniform, coming to snarl at lambs.
>
> "There's work to do!" the officer in charge barked, clapping his gloved hands and then gesturing to the crates we'd unloaded. "Come on! Get a move on!" He fired his orders like cannon balls, and we dispersed frantically to do as he said. "If they're not all unpacked by nightfall, no one eats."

What impressions does the writer create of the characters in these lines?

You must refer to the language used in the text to support your answer, using relevant subject terminology.

Q2 Read the following extract from a piece of travel writing.

> The streets of Kuala Lumpur are a labyrinth of lost lanes, back-streets, dead-ends and alleys, which twist and turn and double back on themselves, constantly trying to bewilder the unaccustomed traveller. An apparently infinite series of haphazard side streets break out from the main street of the Chinatown area, like snakes winding across the desert. On every corner hang the pungent but irresistible smells of food stalls offering a cornucopia of exotic cuisines. Heavy trucks rumble past impatiently, whilst thousands of scooters whine and buzz like a swarm of bees, honking horns and hurling out exhaust fumes that stubbornly stagnate in the desperately hot air. The heat is relentless. Even standing still in the shade I can feel the sweat gathering on my forehead.
>
> In search of a bit of peace from the incessant heat and choking fumes, I make my way to the city centre park. Here, neat pathways wind their way leisurely through immaculate green lawns. On every side of the park, glimmering steel skyscrapers tower into the sky, peering down at the people walking below. It's like being surrounded by a giant metal rainforest, thronging with life.

How does the writer show that Kuala Lumpur is an exciting and overwhelming place to be?

You should comment on:
- what the writer says to influence readers;
- their use of language, tone and structure.

Exam-Style Questions

Q3 Read the following extracts.

19th-Century Letter
Dear Jane,
    I have arrived at my lodgings in Ware. They are satisfactory, if not impressive — the room must once have been decorated in good taste, but alas, it is the good taste of a bygone age. Nevertheless, the room is clean, tidy and of a good size. As I had expected, the mattress was not of the standard I am accustomed to (nor, for that matter, was the limited refreshment offered by the kitchens), but for a short stay, it will suffice.

21st-Century Review
The room smelt like its window hadn't been opened for about a century. The wallpaper was peeling. The carpet was a battlefield between all sorts of suspicious stains. Given the state of the rest of the room, I doubted that the 'fresh' bedding was clean, but it was the mattress that really drew my attention — it was like something from a Victorian prison cell, barely a few inches thick.

Both of these texts are about staying in new rooms. Compare the following:

- the writers' attitudes to their rooms;
- how they get across their views.

You must use the text to support your comments and make it clear which text you are referring to.

Q4 Read the following extract from a short story.

    "Howard, you made it!" Percy beamed, ushering me through the doors of his mansion. "Come in, come in — you don't want to miss a minute of this party; I promise you, it's my best yet!"
    He hastened me through the marble hallway towards the ballroom. I could already hear the thumping of music and the hum of voices. As the golden doors were opened, the noise hit me like a wave. The room was thronged with hundreds of guests, and they were all joking, laughing, making introductions. Their voices wove together into a single, undulating buzz of talk. Beyond their voices was the exuberant playing of the live band; drums and saxophones adding bass and melody to the already throbbing noise. There were other sounds too — the clinking of glasses, the occasional popping of champagne corks followed by cheers.
    And the colours! The men were all in tuxedos, cutting sharp lines of white and black, while the women were shimmering in silks of every colour — emerald and scarlet, gold and violet, cobalt and cerise. Lights glittered from the chandeliers, sparkling on the women's jewellery and the martini glasses and the silverware. The ballroom had become a never-ending kaleidoscope of wealth.

"The writer of this extract uses descriptive language very successfully. The reader really feels like they're at the party." To what extent do you agree with this statement?

You should write about:

- your own impressions of the scene;
- how the writer has created these impressions.

You must refer to the text to support your answer.

Narrative Viewpoint

Literature will always have a narrator — a voice that is telling the story.

The **Narrative Viewpoint** is usually quite **Easy** to spot

1) A first-person narrator tells the story using words like 'I', 'we' and 'me'. A first-person narrator is often one of the characters, telling the reader directly about their feelings and experiences.

> *I stood on the fringes of the stage, waiting my turn, fear coursing through my veins.* A first-person narrator establishes a stronger, more personal connection with the reader.

2) A second-person narrator tells the story using words like 'you'. A second-person narrator talks as if the reader ('you') is one of the characters.

> *You turn your head to see her walking towards you. Your heart begins to race.* A second-person narrator makes the reader 'feel' what the character is feeling.

3) A third-person narrator is not one of the characters. They tell the story using words like 'he' and 'she' to talk about the characters.

> *Jo's elated expression could mean only one thing: she had got a place at medical school.* A third-person narrator has a more detached viewpoint.

Some third-person narrators are omniscient — they know what all the characters are thinking. Others are limited — they only know what one character is thinking.

4) When writing about a narrator, think about how reliable they are. You might not be able to trust them fully if they don't know something, or if they're trying to affect the reader in some way.

Think about how the **Narrator Presents** the **Characters**

PAPER 1

> | 0 | 5 | "In this passage, the writer presents Alice as an annoying character."
>
> To what extent do you agree with this view?

Uses 'she' and is separate to the characters, so it's a third-person narrator.

> Faiza was walking down the corridor when she noticed that Alice was walking towards her. Faiza sighed, rolled her eyes and braced herself.
> "Hi Faiza!" chirped Alice, with her typically exhausting optimism, "I hope I'll see you at the party later!"
> Faiza's face contorted into an obviously forced smile as she nodded sharply.

Think carefully about how the narrator's perspective is being used to affect the reader.

I strongly agree with the evaluation. **The writer has used the narrator's perspective to present Alice as annoying,** despite her actions. Everything she does is positive: she is bright, friendly, optimistic and simply invites Faiza to a party. The narrator presents her optimism as "typically exhausting" though, so her actions come across to the reader as tiresome, rather than positive. **This is reinforced by the narrator's heavy focus on Faiza's expressions,** which all betray her personal dislike for Alice: she "rolled" her eyes and had a "forced smile".

Link your points together to give a really detailed analysis of what the writer has done.

Get to know these different narrative viewpoints...

It can be quite easy to forget about the narrator, because they're often not one of the characters directly involved in the story. But try to think about how they talk, and whether you can trust what they tell you.

Structure — Non-Fiction Texts

Structure is the way a writer organises their ideas within a text. On this page, there's some information about how non-fiction texts use structure — turn over to find out more about structure in fiction texts.

Structure can help to Achieve the writer's Purpose

Writing to Argue or Persuade

- When writing to argue or persuade, a writer may organise their points to gradually build up to a powerful conclusion. E.g. they might start with statistics, then build up to more emotive points.

- A writer might also use a counter-argument, where they will introduce the opposite viewpoint to their own, then explain why they disagree with it in order to build support for their own argument.

- They could also repeat specific words, sentences or ideas in order to emphasise important points.

Writing to Inform or Advise

- When writing to inform or advise, a writer will use a logical structure so that the information is clear and the reader can easily follow their advice.

- They could break up information so that it's less intimidating for the reader by using lots of paragraphs or numbered points.

- They could also include an introduction and a conclusion, to make their advice clear.

Think about how the Text has been Organised

PAPER 2

1 2 | How does the writer of this speech persuade the reader to eat more healthily?

This single-word paragraph helps to persuade the reader by emphasising the strength of the writer's emotions.

This paragraph introduces a new idea — a solution to the problems presented.

The first and last paragraphs start in the same way. This encourages the reader to think about how their opinion has changed.

> As a nation, we have a problem. A recent survey has revealed that a mere 30% of people regularly eat the full five portions of fruit and vegetables that our bodies require daily; a shocking 25% said that they didn't eat any fruit and vegetables at all on a day-to-day basis.
>
> Outrageous.
>
> How have we let this happen? It is simply astonishing that we've fallen into such bad eating habits; simply unforgiveable that we're teaching our children to rely on junk food and sugary rubbish instead of loading them up with the nutrients they require.
>
> It's time to make a change. I'm encouraging everybody to make a tiny tweak to their daily routine. You can make the decision to drop unhealthy, sugar-laden snacks in favour of a juicy apple or crunchy celery stick. You can make a difference to your health, and set a good example to the people around you.
>
> As a nation, perhaps we've gone a little astray, but I don't think it's too late to change our ways. If we work together, we can kick sugary snacks out of our lives, and embrace healthy living for a better future.

The text starts with facts and statistics to establish an authoritative tone and gain the reader's trust, then goes on to explain the author's opinions.

Repetition is used in these paragraphs to emphasise the writer's point of view and make the speech more memorable for the reader.

Structure is used to have an effect on the reader, just like language...

Structure plays a huge part in every text you read, so you'll need to really get to grips with how it works. Think about the way the writer organises their ideas, and the order in which they're presented to the reader.

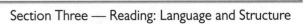

Structure — Fiction Texts

Now that you've got to grips with the structure of non-fiction texts, have a look at these two pages — they're all about how writers use structure in fiction texts, like the one you'll get in paper 1, section A.

Fiction texts use **Structure** to **Entertain** their **Audience**

1) In <u>fiction</u> texts, writers will structure their work in a way they think will <u>entertain</u> the reader. For example:

- Texts with a <u>linear</u> structure are arranged <u>chronologically</u> — events are described in the order in which they happened, and the text <u>flows</u> naturally from <u>beginning</u> to <u>middle</u> to <u>end</u>. They will often engage the reader's interest by <u>building</u> towards some form of <u>climax</u>.

- Texts with a <u>non-linear</u> structure are ordered in a way that makes the text <u>interesting</u>, rather than in chronological order. They might include things like <u>flashbacks</u>, changes in <u>perspective</u> (using different narrators) or <u>time shifts</u>.

2) Whenever you write about structure, you need to show <u>how</u> the writer has used structure to produce a particular effect on the <u>reader</u>.

Writers use **Structure** to **Focus** the reader's **Attention**

One of the easiest ways to write about <u>structure</u> is to think about how the writer is <u>directing</u> your <u>attention</u> as you read. There are lots of ways a writer can do this, for example:

- The writer might draw the reader in by <u>describing</u> something <u>general</u>, then <u>narrow</u> their <u>focus</u> down to something more <u>specific</u>.

- The writer could <u>describe</u> things along a <u>journey</u> and make you feel as if you are travelling with them. This might involve moving from the <u>outside</u> to the <u>inside</u> or just from one place to another.

- A text might start with <u>description</u> and then move on to <u>dialogue</u>. This would shift your focus from <u>setting</u> to <u>characters</u>.

- Often, a writer will use a <u>new paragraph</u> to start a <u>new topic</u>. This could be a <u>smooth</u> transition, or it could have a <u>jarring</u> effect that draws the reader's attention to a particular part of the text.

The **Narrative Viewpoint** will **Affect** the **Structure**

1) The <u>narrator</u> controls what the reader <u>sees</u> and what <u>information</u> they <u>receive</u>, so different <u>narrators</u> will have different <u>effects</u> on the <u>structure</u> of a text:

- A <u>third-person</u> narrator (see p.50) will often have an <u>overall</u> view of the story, so the structure might <u>skip around</u> to cover lots of <u>different</u> events.

- For texts with a <u>first-person</u> narrator, the structure will probably <u>follow</u> that character's experiences quite <u>closely</u>.

2) A narrator might also <u>withhold</u> some information to create <u>tension</u>, or they could <u>skip</u> over certain parts of a story because they are <u>biased</u>.

3) Look out for texts that have <u>more than one</u> narrator. This might mean that the structure <u>jumps around</u> or alternates between the different <u>perspectives</u>.

Structure — Fiction Texts

Think about **What** the writer wants the **Reader** to **Focus On**

| 0 | 4 | How does the writer make these lines interesting for the reader? |

The extract begins by focusing the reader's attention on the setting.

> The mountain looked a little mysterious in the half-light of the dusky evening. Its snow-capped peak stood alert, bathing in the dying embers of the setting sun. From there, my eye was drawn to the narrow path that wound its way precariously down past the dark woods and craggy outcrops of the mountain face. I traced the weaving path all the way down, until it vanished behind the spire of a magnificent church that loomed over the town nestled at the foot of the mountain.

The 'narrow path' is used as a device to lead the reader's focus to the town below the mountains.

The one-line paragraph grabs the reader's attention by providing a contrast to the long descriptive paragraph before it.

> This was the town of my youth.

> This was the town where I had taken my first steps. This was the town where I had been to school, where I had battled through those tough transition years of teenage angst and, finally, where I had first fallen in love. It was permeated with memories of childhood games and, later in my adolescence, secret late-night trysts.

This time-shift switches the reader's attention from the setting to the narrator's childhood, which allows the reader to learn more about the character and her story.

> I crossed the road and entered the alley that would take me deeper into the warren of streets that wound their way around the foot of the imposing church. When I finally emerged into the square, I was assaulted by a barrage of sights and smells that instantly took me all the way back to my youth.

The final sentence leads into the next paragraph so that the time-shift doesn't jar too much, and enables the reader to follow the action easily.

> Immediately, I was back under the oak tree, crouching silently next to my best friend Mirela. We were hiding from James Cotton, and it was a matter of grave honour that we preserved our hiding place.

This text has a non-linear structure — it skips forwards and backwards in time.

Paragraphs are used here to help the reader follow both the narrator's thoughts and her journey. They show changes in topic, time, character or place.

> Back then, a game of hide and seek was no mere playground triviality. It was a fierce battle between the sexes, a passionately fought war between two equally resolute forces. We spent endless days squirrelled away in the nooks and crannies of the town we knew like the back of our hand, listening out warily for the tell-tale scramble of footsteps that meant James had found our hiding place.

This long sentence emphasises the 'endless days' of the narrator's childhood.

> Both Mirela and I were fascinated with James: he was old for his age, smart and funny. Obviously, at that age, this fascination manifested itself as bitter hatred. For me, the coyness would come later, at around the same time as the feelings of claustrophobia and a strong yearning for the big city. Mirela hadn't felt the same longing for the metropolis as I had, but she had discovered the coyness that would replace the naive and innocent feud. She had stayed here and built a life for herself.

The text's structure takes the reader along with the narrator on her journey through the town. It takes the reader on a journey through the narrator's childhood too.

> Tomorrow morning I was to attend the wedding at which she would become Mrs Cotton.

This single-sentence paragraph suggests that the wedding is going to be an important event in the story.

> The tolling of the church bells brought me back to the present with a start. I needed to hurry if I was to get to my parents' house before dinnertime. With a sigh of nostalgia, I turned away from the old oak tree, and began the final leg of the journey back to my former home...

EXAM TIP

You may need to dig a little deeper when analysing structure...

It can be tricky to think of something insightful to say about linear texts because there aren't any time-shifts or flashbacks. If you're stuck, think about how the writer is directing your attention.

Sentence Forms

Writing about the effects of different sentence forms will earn you marks in questions about both structure and language, so it's well worth reading up on the next two pages.

Sentences are made up of **Clauses**

The subject is the person or thing doing the verb.

1) A clause is a part of a sentence that has a subject and a verb. A clause usually makes sense on its own.

2) A single clause on its own is called a simple sentence.

> *The sky was grey and sombre.* This is a single clause that is also a simple sentence. It has a subject ('The sky') and a verb ('was').

3) Simple sentences can be used to explain something clearly and simply. They are also often used to create a sharp or abrupt tone that keeps the reader engaged or creates tension.

4) A compound sentence has two main clauses, linked by a conjunction like 'or', 'but' or 'and'. Both clauses have to be able to make sense on their own. For example:

> *The sky was grey and sombre, and the rain lashed at our faces.* Writers can use compound sentences to do things like expand on their initial statement, creating more detailed and interesting descriptions.

5) Complex sentences have two or more clauses, but only one of them needs to make sense on its own.

> *Above the sleepy town, the sky was grey and sombre.* → This is a complex sentence — 'Above the sleepy town' wouldn't work as a sentence on its own. This clause could go either before or after the main clause. Writers often create interest by using complex sentences to break up the rhythm of a text.

6) Writers use a variety of sentence forms to achieve different effects and keep the reader interested.

There are **Four Main Types** of sentence

1) Different types of sentences have different purposes:

- Statements deliver information, e.g. 'The referee made the decision.' They can be found in all texts, but they are particularly common in informative texts like newspaper articles, reports and reviews.

- Questions ask the reader something, e.g. 'What would you do in my situation?' They don't always require an answer — sometimes they are just there to encourage us to think about something.

- Orders, or commands, tell us to do something, e.g. 'Consider the effects of this in the long-term.' They often use imperative verbs (verbs that give an instruction, like 'remember', 'think about' or 'go').

- Exclamations convey strong emotions, e.g. 'This is outrageous!' or 'This cannot be allowed to continue!' They usually end with an exclamation mark, and they're common in persuasive texts.

2) For the reading questions, it's a good idea to think about how and why writers have used particular types of sentence — bear in mind that different sentence types are suited to different purposes.

Sentence Forms

Writers use **Different Sentence Forms** to **Interest** the reader

1) Varying the <u>length</u> of sentences can create different <u>effects</u>. Here are a couple of <u>examples</u>:

> These are just examples — the effects of different sentence lengths will vary from text to text.

> *The sky was growing darker. I couldn't see where I was going. I stumbled.* Short simple sentences can be used to <u>build tension</u> or to create a <u>worried</u> and <u>confused</u> tone.

> *I waited excitedly at the foot of the stairs, listening to the footsteps above, thinking about the afternoon ahead, pacing the hall and counting down the minutes until we could set off.* A longer, complex sentence could be used to give the impression of <u>time dragging</u>.

2) The <u>order</u> of words within sentences can also be chosen to create an <u>effect</u>. For example:

> *I had <u>never</u> seen such chaos <u>before</u>.*
>
> *<u>Never before</u> had I seen such chaos.* Writers sometimes use <u>inversion</u> (<u>altering</u> the normal <u>word order</u>) to change the <u>emphasis</u> in a text. Here, inversion helps to emphasise the phrase '<u>Never before</u>'.

3) If you notice something about the way a writer has used sentences, don't just identify it — you need to <u>analyse</u> the <u>effects</u> to show how they <u>influence</u> the reader.

Comment on the **Effects** of different **Sentence Forms**

PAPER 1

| 0 | 3 | What impression do you get of the narrator's feelings from these lines? |

This is a long sentence that leaves the reader breathless by the end. It emphasises the feeling of weariness that the narrator is describing.

The use of a colon shows that there is going to be some form of explanation. This highlights the move away from unexplained short simple sentences.

It was late evening by the time I returned home from the shops, tired and weary from barging my way past all the desperate Christmas Eve shoppers. It had been a long day, and I was ready for a relaxing bath and a long sleep. It wasn't until I was halfway up the path that I noticed the front door was ajar. **My heart began** beating wildly inside my chest as I hesitantly advanced towards the door. **My hands began** to shake. **My mind began** conjuring apparitions of the unspeakable horrors that could be lurking inside. On reaching the door, I took a deep breath, collected my senses and stepped across the threshold. Everything was quiet and still. I crossed the hall and put down my shopping. **Everything looked normal. Nothing was out of place. Suddenly I heard a noise above me. Someone was upstairs. I gasped.** But then a change came over me: my fear **had turned to resolute anger.** Seldom **had I** experienced such intense fury in all my life. There was an intruder in my house, and they had no right to be there. I made for the stairs.

The repetition in the sentence beginnings 'My heart began', 'My hands began' and 'My mind began' gives emphasis to the physical effects of the narrator's fear.

Short, simple sentences are used to reinforce the narrator's feelings of dread.

This inversion disrupts the usual word order and focuses the reader's attention on the narrator's anger.

This longer sentence marks a change in tone from fear to anger.

Make sure you learn the terms for different sentences...

It'll help you if you can discuss the effects of sentence forms in the language and structure questions, so remember to learn the technical terms for different forms and types of sentences.

Presentation

The exams are mostly focused on the effects of language and structure, but some texts may also have presentational features that you could comment on. Here's some information on features to look out for.

Think about the **Effect** of **Pictures**

1) Texts often use <u>pictures</u> to <u>illustrate</u> what they're about.

2) Sometimes pictures are used to emphasise a <u>feeling</u>. For example, photos of the effects of war make us see how <u>horrible</u> it must be.

3) Pictures can be specially <u>selected</u> to emphasise <u>one particular feeling</u> instead of others. E.g. a writer could make sure there are no <u>hopeful</u> photos of people being rescued in a war — that way we're <u>only shown</u> how horrible it is.

4) Pictures often have <u>captions</u> with them — a short bit of text that helps the reader to <u>understand</u> what the picture shows.

Headlines and Subheadings help to Focus the reader's Attention

1) Headlines tell you, very <u>briefly</u>, what a newspaper or magazine article is <u>about</u>.

2) They try to capture the reader's <u>interest</u>, so that the reader <u>wants</u> to continue reading the text. To do this, they might use <u>humour</u> or language techniques such as <u>onomatopoeia</u> or <u>hyperbole</u>:

> *MEMBERS MOURN AS CRICKET CLUB CREMATED*
>
> *Residents of Halsington are said to be "in shock" after a major fire swept through the cricket club.* This headline uses <u>alliteration</u> and the <u>semantic field</u> of <u>funerals</u> (see p.35) to grab the reader's <u>attention</u> and make the article seem <u>interesting</u>.

3) <u>Subheadings</u> can be used to <u>split</u> a text up, so that the material is presented in <u>smaller</u> sections that are easier for the reader to <u>take in</u>.

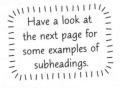
Have a look at the next page for some examples of subheadings.

4) Subheadings aim to <u>summarise</u> a part of the text, so they're usually quite <u>concise</u>, but they can also be <u>interesting</u> or <u>funny</u>, which encourages the reader to continue reading.

Bullet Points and Numbered Lists help Break Information Up

1) <u>Bullet points</u> and <u>numbered lists</u> are often used when writers want to give you <u>lots of information</u>, e.g. when writing to <u>advise</u> or <u>inform</u>.

2) They separate complex information into <u>concise</u> points to make it easier to <u>understand</u> and <u>remember</u>.

3) Numbered lists are most commonly used when information needs to be read in a <u>specific order</u>:

> *1. Preheat the oven to 200°C.*
> *2. Mix the butter, eggs, sugar and flour in a large bowl.*
> *3. Pour the mixture into a cake tin and bake until golden brown.* This uses <u>numbered points</u> to give step-by-step instructions that are <u>easy</u> for the reader to <u>follow</u>.

4) Bullet points are often used when the order of the points <u>isn't as important</u>.

> *To stay healthy, you need to:*
> * *Drink plenty of water.*
> * *Eat lots of fruit and vegetables.* It doesn't <u>matter</u> what <u>order</u> these points are in, but the <u>bullet points</u> break the information up <u>clearly</u> so it stands out to the reader.

Presentation

Write about how **Presentation Affects** the **Reader**

| 1 | 2 | The author of this magazine article is trying to persuade the reader to exercise more. How does she try to do this? |

This uses a title to immediately suggest to the reader that keeping fit is 'easy'.

KEEPING FIT — THE EASY WAY

Exercise is important for your health, but nowadays our time and budget are often limited. Fortunately, there are many cheap, simple and fun ways to keep fit.

WALK THE WALK

Walking costs you nothing, and it doesn't require too much spare time. You could try:

- Walking to a friend's house instead of asking for a lift.
- Planning a longer route to a destination you already walk to.
- Getting off the bus or train a few stops early and walking the rest of the way.

Bullet points are used to break the information up for the reader, making it more accessible.

Interesting subheadings are used to organise the text and hold the reader's interest.

PEDAL POWER

If you own a bike, cycling is an excellent way to keep fit. Look at your council's website to see if there are cycle routes nearby, or plan a safe route on your local roads.

DANCE THE NIGHT AWAY

Dancing can help to maintain your fitness and improve your coordination, regardless of your skill level. Try looking for tutorial videos on the Internet or local classes to help you learn something new.

This includes a picture, which adds interest for the reader and illustrates a point being made in the text.

YOUR TURN...

These are just a few ideas; there are many more options available. Whether it's skipping, skating or salsa, there will certainly be something for you.

This explains why the text's presentation is significant.

The writer uses a short headline to introduce the article and **draw attention to the idea that keeping fit can be "easy"**. The title is also set in capital letters and bold type, so that the idea really stands out. **This might persuade the reader to exercise more by immediately and clearly suggesting that it isn't too difficult to do.**

Remember to link your points back to the question.

You don't need to give a detailed description of a picture — just make it clear how it affects the reader.

The article also includes an appealing image of a cyclist at sunset, which helps to persuade the reader by suggesting that cycling is a pleasant activity that they would enjoy doing. The image also breaks up the text, which makes the article look more interesting and less intimidating. This might encourage the reader to continue reading the article and therefore make them more likely to be persuaded to exercise more.

EXAM TIP

Don't spend too long describing the details of an image...

Be careful when writing about presentational devices. It's good to discuss them in your answer — just don't get carried away describing a picture when you could be analysing the effect it has.

Worked Answer

Right, it's time for another worked answer...

0 4 Read the following extract. It is from the opening to a short story.

> The theatre hummed with expectant conversation as the spectators began to fill the stalls. The red velvet seats and gentle golden lighting gave the impression of being caught in the centre of a giant ruby. There was a magical feeling, as if everyone knew they were going to witness something spectacular that night, and eyes kept flickering over to the theatre drapes, wondering when the show would begin.
>
> Backstage, biting his fingernails down to the nail-bed, was the one they were all waiting for. Mikhail had been told by everyone he met that he was the greatest tenor of all time. Conductors had shed a tear when he sang, audiences had wept openly. But that never stopped him from feeling sick with nerves before a performance. What if his voice faltered? What if he forgot the words? What if he disappointed them all?
>
> "Sixty seconds to curtain," the stage manager called to him. Mikhail took a deep breath. His palms were damp with sweat. His legs felt like jelly. He didn't know if he was ready for this.

How does the writer make these lines tense and dramatic?

You should write about:

- the writer's use of language to make these lines tense and dramatic;
- how the structure of these lines makes them tense and dramatic;
- the effects on the reader.

You must refer to the text to support your answer, using relevant subject terminology.

long sentences build anticipation, gradually become shorter to create tension;

vivid description to bring sense of exclusivity and grandeur — drama;

changes in focus — time still passing;

sensory language to show Mikhail's nerves

You **don't** need to make a <u>detailed plan</u> for this type of question, but <u>quickly</u> jotting down your <u>ideas</u> (like this) can be helpful.

The reference to <u>different sentence lengths</u> addresses the <u>second bullet point</u> in the question.

This example is fine, but the quote could be <u>shorter</u>.

<u>The writer uses a variety of language and structure features to make these lines tense and dramatic.</u> Tension is built gradually throughout the extract by the writer's <u>use of a selection of different sentence types and lengths.</u> The first paragraph features a long, complex sentence which tells the reader that <u>"There was a magical feeling, as if everyone knew they were going to witness something spectacular that night..."</u> This sets the scene by focusing on the waiting audience, which establishes a sense of anticipation regarding the show. <u>As the extract</u>

Nice opening — it gets <u>straight</u> to the <u>point</u>.

Worked Answer

This point is quite <u>underdeveloped</u> — you should explain how the shorter sentences increase the pace.

Always keep the <u>focus</u> of the question in mind.

continues, <u>the sentences get shorter, such as "His legs felt like jelly." The shorter sentences help to increase the extract's pace and build tension and drama for the reader.</u>

In the first paragraph, <u>vivid language</u> heightens <u>the drama of the passage</u> and makes the spectacle of the occasion clear to the reader. The writer likens the scene to being <u>"caught in the centre of a giant ruby"</u>. This imagery suggests rarity and extravagance, which makes the reader aware of how exclusive the performance is. This further increases the sense of pressure and tension within the lines, especially when combined with the writer's description of Mikhail "feeling sick with nerves".

In addition to this, at several points throughout the extract the writer uses changes in perspective to add tension. For example, the switch to the stage manager's dialogue in the third paragraph interrupts Mikhail's panicked thought process from the previous paragraph. By <u>reminding the reader</u> that time is still passing and that Mikhail's performance is rapidly approaching, the <u>tension in the extract is increased</u>.

The reference to <u>language</u> addresses the <u>first bullet point</u> in the question.

<u>Support</u> your points with short quotations or references to the text.

This question type is all about the <u>effect</u> on the <u>reader</u>.

This is all about <u>sensory language</u> — you could use the technical term here.

<u>The writer's use of description based on the senses</u> at the end of the extract brings the tension to its highest level. The statement that Mikhail's "palms were damp with sweat" helps the reader clearly imagine the stress that Mikhail is feeling. Readers could perhaps relate to this experience, and might begin to feel nervous too. This personal element encourages the reader to become more engaged in the story and makes the sense of drama and tension at the event very clear to them.

- This answer has explored a variety of language and structural features — such as changes in perspective and imagery— and explained their effects on the reader. It also backs up these points with suitable examples.

- To get the top marks, this answer could be improved by:

  - keeping quotations precise

  - using a few more technical terms, e.g. sensory language

  - making sure all points are fully developed by including a bit more detail.

Exam-Style Questions

You should know the drill by now — use these exam-style questions to help you practise for the real thing.

Q1 This is the ending to a short story. Joan is eighty-six years old, and one of the nurses from her care home has volunteered to take her to the beach.

> They arrived shortly before lunchtime. The seagulls squawked noisily overhead, swooping and circling, bright as doves against the blue sky. The nurse pushed the wheelchair down the boardwalk. Looking out over the sand and the grey-green sea, Joan was transfixed.
>
> The first time she had been to the beach was as a little girl, shortly before the war broke out. It had been a hot day. The beach was full of people sprawled on multicoloured deck chairs and picnic blankets, lending the scene a carnival feel. She remembered the smell of the water as she raced into the sea for the first time. She remembered the feeling of damp sand between her fingers and toes, and how the sea salt had dried into tiny crystals on her skin. Her mother had packed a picnic of hard-boiled eggs and potato salad. It had been the best day of her life so far, and as her father had bundled her into a towel, tired and sun-soaked, ready to go home, she had already been looking forward to the next visit.
>
> Now Joan watched the children race delightedly across the sand like she had done. Her nurse bought her fish and chips for lunch. Joan bought sticks of rock for her great-grandchildren. As the sun was going down, and they headed back to the car, Joan looked back over her shoulder. She knew there wouldn't be a next visit — but she didn't mind. She had seen the sea again.

How does the writer make these lines interesting for the reader? You should write about:

- the writer's use of language to make these lines interesting;
- how the structure of these lines makes them interesting;
- the effects on the reader.

Q2 Read the following letter to the editor of the *Daily Muncaster* local newspaper.

> Dear Sir,
>
> I was frankly horrified to read your article about the new soft drink 'Swampy Water' being served in the tuck shop at Muncaster Primary School. This dangerous fad for drinking green, slimy water is clearly idiotic.
>
> Firstly, young children may become confused and think it acceptable to drink real swamp water. I know from my time in the Territorial Army that this would be an ill-advised and perhaps even fatal decision. Secondly, 'Swampy Water' is full of unhealthy sugar and additives — how else would it acquire that lurid green tinge? Finally, the drink is expensive, which means children don't have sufficient funds to purchase the normal, healthy snacks that any sane parent would endorse.
>
> To conclude, it is my firm belief that 'Swampy Water' should be immediately removed from the tuck shop at Muncaster Primary School.
>
> Yours faithfully,
> Gerry Bowness

The writer is trying to argue that 'Swampy Water' should be banned. How does he try to do this?

You should comment on:

- what he says to influence the reader;
- his use of language, tone and structure.

Revision Summary

If you've got to grips with the section, this page will be a breeze. Don't move on until you can do it all.

- Try these questions and <u>tick off each one</u> when you <u>get it right</u>.
- When you've done <u>all the questions</u> under a heading and are <u>completely happy</u> with it, tick it off.

Tone and Style (p.32-35) ☐

1) Are the following definitions for tone or style?
   a) This is the overall way in which the text is written.
   b) This is the feeling the words are written with. ☑

2) Would you expect the register of the following types of writing to be formal or informal?
   a) a job advert for the role of bank manager
   b) a newspaper article reporting on changes to the tax system
   c) an article about mountain biking on a website aimed at teenagers ☑

3) True or false?
   *In your English Language exams, you should comment on
   the effect of individual words and phrases in the text.* ☑

Language (p.38-46) ☐

4) What is the difference between a metaphor and a simile? ☑

5) Which of the following are metaphors and which are similes?
   a) He was as hairy as a dog.
   b) On the racetrack my sister was a whippet.
   c) You look like something the cat dragged in. ☑

6) Why might a writer give the weight of a cruise ship in elephants rather than in tonnes? ☑

7) Ella says "the writer uses personification — he describes the young girl as if she were an animal."
   Why is Ella wrong? ☑

8) Choose an alliterative adjective to go with 'badger' to make the badger sound:
   a) attractive
   b) dangerous ☑

9) Write out three examples of onomatopoeic words. ☑

10) What is irony? ☑

11) What is the main thing you can look at to work out if a writer is being sarcastic? ☑

12) Name three rhetorical techniques. ☑

13) True or false? *It'll always be obvious if a text is biased.* ☑

14) Which word fills in the blank? *Writers often give descriptions based on the five _____.* ☑

Narrative Viewpoint, Structure and Presentation (p.50-57) ☐

15) What are the three types of narrative viewpoint? Write down a brief definition for each one. ☑

16) Give one way structure can be used to achieve the writer's purpose in texts that entertain or argue. ☑

17) Are the following sentences simple, compound or complex?
   a) Gazing longingly out to sea, the sailor dreamed of adventure.
   b) I waited for an hour, but he never arrived.
   c) She listened in shock to the news on the radio. ☑

18) What are the four main types of sentence? ☑

19) Why might a writer use subheadings? ☑

Section Three — Reading: Language and Structure

Writing with Purpose

All writing has a purpose, so you need to make it clear in both your fiction and non-fiction writing.

Structure your writing to **Suit** your **Purpose**

See pages 15-19 for more about writer's purpose.

1) The purpose of your writing might be to <u>inform</u>, <u>advise</u>, <u>argue</u> or <u>persuade</u>, or <u>entertain</u>. It could even be <u>more than one</u> of these.

2) For paper 1, you'll be asked to write <u>creatively</u>, so your purpose should be to <u>entertain</u>.

3) For paper 2, the purpose might be <u>obvious</u>, e.g. you could be asked to write a letter to <u>advise</u> the reader. It can be <u>less obvious</u> though, e.g. you might be asked to "share your views" on a topic, which you could do by writing to <u>argue</u> or <u>persuade</u>.

4) Different purposes will need different <u>structures</u>, so you'll need to think about a <u>structure</u> that will help you achieve your purpose most effectively.

5) You can lay out your structure by writing a <u>plan</u>, so that it stays <u>consistent</u> throughout your answer:

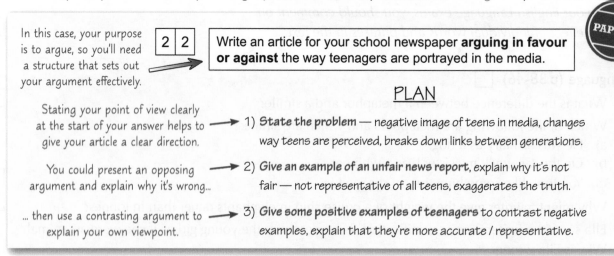

In this case, your purpose is to argue, so you'll need a structure that sets out your argument effectively.

2 2 → Write an article for your school newspaper **arguing in favour or against** the way teenagers are portrayed in the media.

PAPER 2

PLAN

Stating your point of view clearly at the start of your answer helps to give your article a clear direction.

→ 1) **State the problem** — negative image of teens in media, changes way teens are perceived, breaks down links between generations.

You could present an opposing argument and explain why it's wrong...

→ 2) **Give an example of an unfair news report**, explain why it's not fair — not representative of all teens, exaggerates the truth.

... then use a contrasting argument to explain your own viewpoint.

→ 3) **Give some positive examples of teenagers** to contrast negative examples, explain that they're more accurate / representative.

Choose your **Tone**, **Style** and **Register** to match your **Purpose**

See p.32-33 for more on tone, style and register.

1) In order to get good marks, you also need to show that you can <u>adjust</u> your <u>tone</u>, <u>style</u> and <u>register</u> to suit your purpose.

2) For example, an <u>informative</u> text might have a <u>serious</u>, <u>reserved</u> style, with a <u>formal</u> register:

The UK's younger generation show signs of frustration at the way they are perceived. Studies show that up to 95% of 18-24 year-olds feel that their stance on environmentalism is being ignored. 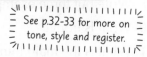 This text uses <u>technical terms</u> and <u>statistics</u> to help clearly inform the reader.

3) A <u>persuasive</u> text needs to be more <u>subjective</u> (based on personal feelings). It might use rhetorical techniques (see p.44) to create a <u>personal</u> tone that involves the reader in a text:

Like me, you must be weary of the incessant criticism. We're intelligent young citizens who understand the issues threatening our planet. Why are we being ignored? This text uses a <u>rhetorical question</u> and the pronouns 'you' and 'we' to <u>involve</u> and <u>persuade</u> its audience.

4) When you adjust your <u>writing</u> to suit your purpose, make sure you're still showing off your ability to use <u>sophisticated vocabulary</u>.

Writing with Purpose

Fiction texts are often written to Entertain

PAPER 1

| 1 | 1 |

*In this section you will be assessed for the quality of your **creative prose writing** skills.*

Choose **one** of the following titles for your writing:

Either, *(a)* Finding Inspiration.
Or, *(b)* Old Friends.
Or, *(c)* Write about a time when you felt frightened.
Or, *(d)* Write a story which ends:
...I'd never been so far from home before,
but now I was extremely glad I went.

You're writing a piece of fiction, so you need to entertain the reader.

This story starts in the middle of the action to grab the reader's interest.

<u>FINDING INSPIRATION</u>

I'd never in my life needed a break so badly. My airless writing room had begun to feel suffocating; so had the frustration of my unending writer's block. I gave up, threw down my pen, and went out for a walk.

My **irritation evaporated** almost immediately into the crisp autumn air. **Buoyed** by the hope of finding inspiration amongst the fiery leaves that surrounded me, I **ambled** contentedly through the silence of the golden wood.

This uses complex sentences to keep the writing style varied.

Figurative language helps the reader to imagine the writer's feelings.

Unusual vocabulary makes your writing more interesting and enjoyable to read.

Non-fiction texts can have a Variety of Purposes

| 2 | 2 |

You have read a magazine article which claims that cosmetic surgery is needless and should be banned.

You have decided to write an article for your local newspaper to share your views on this idea. You could write in favour or against this idea.
Write a lively article for the newspaper giving your views.

In this task, your purpose is to explain your point of view — you could do this by writing to <u>argue</u>.

If you're writing to argue, you could structure your answer by stating an opposing opinion and then counteracting it.

Public consensus has long seen cosmetic surgery as a mere vanity project, a procedure dreamed up by the wealthy to aid their endless pursuit of perfection. **This seems somewhat unfair on the medical establishment.**

In truth, cosmetic surgery sits at the height of medical achievement. Far from being a symptom of a shallow society, cosmetic procedures are a solution: **they offer the chance of a new life**. Plastic surgery has the power to improve lives, something that has always been an important medical objective.

It is time for a sea-change in attitudes to plastic surgery — **it is no longer acceptable** for the world to view with scorn those who have chosen to specialise in the improvement of the human form.

Emotive phrases like this can help to make the audience agree with your viewpoint.

You need to use a confident, assured tone to make your argument convincing.

There are marks available for adapting your writing to fit a purpose...

Don't forget that writing can often have more than one purpose (see p.15) — make sure you think about all the reasons that you're writing, so that you can adapt your style and produce a high-level answer.

Writing for an Audience

For each writing task, you'll need to think about your audience. Your audience is just anyone who's going to hear or read your writing — it doesn't mean you'll have to perform your work.

Work out **Who** the **Audience** is for your writing

1) For the writing questions on both papers, you'll need to write in a way that suits your audience.

2) In paper 1, your creative writing will need to appeal to a general, adult audience.

3) In paper 2, a question might specify a particular audience:

> **2 1** Your local council wants to improve how eco-friendly they are. **Write a report for the members of your local council suggesting ways this might be done.**

Here's the audience — 'the members of your local council'.

PAPER 2

4) However, you might need to work out who your audience is, using clues from the question. The form might give you some ideas:

PAPER 2

> **2 2** You have read a report which claims that students should attend school virtually instead of in person. **Write an article to be published in a broadsheet newspaper giving your views on this idea.**

You're writing a broadsheet newspaper article, so your audience will mostly be well-educated adults.

Choose your **Tone**, **Style** and **Register** to match your **Audience**

1) Once you know who your audience is, you'll need to adapt your tone, style and register so that they're appropriate to the people who will be reading your writing.

2) For example, you might want to consider the age and level of expertise of your audience, as well as your relationship with them.

See p.32-33 for more on tone, style and register.

Age

- If you're addressing a younger audience, you might use a more light-hearted tone and an informal register, with a colloquial or chatty style.

- A formal, serious register that doesn't use any slang might work better for older audiences. You might also use a more complex style than you would for a younger audience.

Relationship with reader

- If you're writing to a familiar audience, like a friend, you might use an informal register, and a friendly tone.

- If you're writing to an unknown audience, it would be better to use an impersonal tone and a formal register.

Expertise

- Different audiences will have different levels of expertise in the subject you're writing about.

- For example, if you're writing a report for a panel of experts, your register should be more formal, with a style that uses more specialised language than if you were writing for a general audience.

3) You should always aim to show your writing skills to the examiner — even if you're writing informally or for a young audience, you still need to make sure you include a range of vocabulary and sentence types.

Writing for an Audience

Fiction Texts need to Engage their Audience

| 1 | 1 | In this section you will be assessed for the quality of your **creative prose writing** skills. |

Choose **one** of the following titles for your writing:

Either, *(a)* The New Shoes.

Or, *(b)* Write about a birthday party.

You'll be given four options in the real exam.

Amelia's eighteenth birthday had truly been a day like no other. It was the day she first met Jack: a tall, handsome stranger dressed in a naval uniform.

Don't be fooled by the intrusion of a charming stranger into this narrative. This is not a romance novel, and Amelia was not Cinderella. Jack was her brother — her long-lost brother, who had left to join the Navy before she had been born, and who returned now with the cowed despondence of a disgraced man.

Amelia could never forget her mother's face as she had opened the door to greet another well-wishing neighbour, only to find her lost son hunched on the doorstep. **Her features appeared to melt, losing all definition as they formed themselves into a canvas over which several emotions flashed.** At first there was shock, which quickly became anger, then relief, and finally, remorse.

Try surprising your audience with something unexpected, e.g. addressing the reader directly.

The writing question in paper 1 won't give a specific audience, so you need to make sure that your writing appeals to a general, adult audience.

An unusual image like this makes the text interesting for the audience.

Non-fiction texts can use a Personal Tone

| 2 | 1 | Your school is worried about the dangers of online bullying. **Write a speech to be given at your school advising teenagers on how to cope with online bullying.** |

In this task, you're writing for a teenage audience, so you'll need to adjust your tone, style and register accordingly.

You're writing to advise teenagers. Use words like "we" and "us" to establish a connection and give your advice calmly, without being patronising.

Every day, most of us use some form of social media to broadcast our identities. We're telling the world, "This is who I am." That's why cyber-bullying, whether it's a public post on social media or a private email from an anonymous source, can be so upsetting — it can feel like your whole identity is being attacked.

There are many different ways to deal with online bullying. The first thing you need to do is report it. You can usually do this on the website itself, but if you don't feel comfortable doing this, you should talk to someone in person.

Your tone should be helpful and friendly, but in this case your register should still be quite formal. Don't use any slang or text speak.

If you find you are the victim of persistent bullying, take steps to block the person who is bullying you from contacting you. It's also a good idea to record the bullying in some way — you could take a screenshot, or even just save the messages somewhere. This will make things much easier to report later.

Show the examiner that you're aware of your audience...

You need to adapt your writing to the audience. When you're writing your answer, try to imagine you're the intended audience so you can make sure you've got the tone, style and register right.

Creative Writing

You need to do some creative writing for paper 1. These pages will give you some techniques you can use to create an effective piece of creative writing. It's a good idea to practise this type of question before the exam.

Grab your Reader's Attention from the Start

1) It's always a good idea to <u>start</u> your writing with an <u>opening sentence</u> that'll make your <u>reader</u> want to <u>carry on</u> reading. For example:

You could start with a <u>direct address</u> to the reader:

> *Everybody has a bad day now and again, don't they? Well, I'm going to tell you about a day that was much, much worse than your worst day ever.*

Or you could try a description of a particularly <u>unusual character</u>:

> *Humphrey Ward was, without a shadow of a doubt, the most brilliant (and most cantankerous) banana thief in the country.*

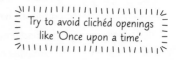
Try to avoid clichéd openings like 'Once upon a time'.

2) If you start your writing in the <u>middle of the action</u>, it'll create a <u>fast-paced</u> atmosphere that makes the reader want to find out <u>what happens next</u>:

> *I couldn't believe it. He was gone. "He must be here," I thought to myself as I went through the shed, desperately throwing aside box after box. It was no use. Tanmay had run away, and it was all my fault.*

3) This example <u>explains</u> some of what's happening after a few sentences, which keeps up the <u>fast pace</u> of the narrative — so the text stays <u>interesting</u>.

4) You could also try <u>prolonging</u> the mystery to create <u>tension</u> in your narrative. Just make sure you <u>reveal</u> what's going on before it gets <u>confusing</u>.

5) However you start your writing, you need to make sure it's <u>engaging</u> and <u>entertaining</u> for the reader — so use interesting <u>language</u> and don't <u>waffle</u>.

Try to Build the Tension from the Start

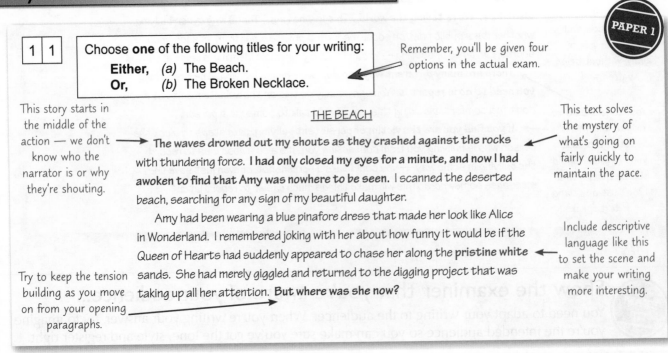

PAPER 1

| 1 | 1 | Choose **one** of the following titles for your writing:
Either, *(a)* The Beach.
Or, *(b)* The Broken Necklace. |

Remember, you'll be given four options in the actual exam.

This story starts in the middle of the action — we don't know who the narrator is or why they're shouting.

<u>THE BEACH</u>

The waves drowned out my shouts as they crashed against the rocks with thundering force. I had only closed my eyes for a minute, and now I had awoken to find that Amy was nowhere to be seen. I scanned the deserted beach, searching for any sign of my beautiful daughter.

Amy had been wearing a blue pinafore dress that made her look like Alice in Wonderland. I remembered joking with her about how funny it would be if the Queen of Hearts had suddenly appeared to chase her along the **pristine white** sands. She had merely giggled and returned to the digging project that was taking up all her attention. **But where was she now?**

This text solves the mystery of what's going on fairly quickly to maintain the pace.

Include descriptive language like this to set the scene and make your writing more interesting.

Try to keep the tension building as you move on from your opening paragraphs.

Creative Writing

Make your **Language** and **Narrative Viewpoint** fit the **Task**

1) Different <u>word choices</u> will have different <u>effects</u>, so you'll need to pick vocabulary that creates the right <u>tone</u> for your story. For example:

> *The door screeched open and I carefully entered the dingy cellar. Shadows cast by my torch leapt up at me through the gloom.*

Words like '<u>screeched</u>', '<u>dingy</u>' and '<u>gloom</u>' make this writing sound <u>spooky</u>.

> *I burst noisily through the thicket of trees and sprinted towards the shore. The men were still chasing me, bellowing threats.*

Words like '<u>burst</u>', '<u>sprinted</u>' and '<u>chasing</u>' make this writing sound <u>exciting</u> and <u>dramatic</u>.

2) You also need to think about what <u>narrative viewpoint</u> you're going to use (see p.50).

3) A <u>first-person narrator</u> uses the pronouns 'I' and 'we', as they're usually one of the <u>characters</u> in the story.

> *I quickly scanned the book for anything that might help. My heart was racing; I knew I needed to work fast.*

The first-person narrative makes things more <u>dramatic</u> by helping the reader to <u>imagine</u> the story is happening to them.

4) A <u>third-person narrator</u> uses words like 'he' and 'she' to talk <u>about</u> the characters from a <u>separate</u> viewpoint.

> *Shamil lit the bonfire carefully, then retreated back a few metres as the feeble fire began to crackle and spit.*

The narrator isn't part of the story. This creates <u>distance</u>, as the narrative voice and the characters are <u>separate</u> from each other.

Use **Descriptive Techniques** to make your text **Engaging**

> | 1 | 1 | Choose **one** of the following titles for your writing:
> **Either,** *(a)* Write about a time when you visited a friend.
> **Or,** *(b)* The Camp.

It's important to show off your descriptive skills to the examiner — interesting vocabulary and imagery can help you achieve this.

Combine visual imagery with other senses to help the reader imagine they are there with the narrator.

<u>THE CAMP</u>

The sun dipped low beneath the looming, dusky sky. Its daytime glory was reduced to the fading flicker of a tiny ember that only just protruded above the dark horizon.

Down in the valley, the camp hummed with activity: **people milled about like ants**, erecting tents, cooking meals and tending the fire, the smoke from which **crept stealthily** up the side of the mound, eventually reaching **the rider's** nostrils and filling him with the **warming aromas of home**.

A glance beyond the confines of the camp revealed the open plains beyond, as they bathed in **the warmth of the dying light**. Come nightfall, these plains would transform from places of refuge into discordant wastelands, answerable only to the laws of nature.

Using figurative language, like similes and personification, will help to make your text more engaging.

This text uses a third-person narrator, so the narrative isn't limited to the rider's perspective.

Creative Writing

It's Important to write a Good Ending

1) It's important that you <u>finish</u> your writing well — you want to leave the examiner with a <u>great impression</u> of your writing abilities.

2) Here are some <u>examples</u> of different ways that you could <u>end</u> your writing:

> * You could finish with an unexpected <u>plot twist</u> that will <u>shock</u> the reader.
> * You could show the <u>main character</u> coming to some kind of <u>realisation</u>.
> * You could create a <u>cliffhanger</u> ending by finishing with a <u>question</u>. This will leave the reader thinking about what will happen <u>next</u>.
> * You could have a <u>neat</u>, <u>happy ending</u> that will <u>satisfy</u> the reader.

Under absolutely no circumstances use the ending, "And it was all a dream."

3) If you find you're running out of time, think up a <u>quick ending</u> — make sure you show how the story ends, and finish with a short, <u>punchy</u> line.

Try to make your Ending as Powerful as possible

PAPER 1

| 1 1 | Choose **one** of the following titles for your writing:
Either, *(a)* The Decision.
Or, *(b)* The House on the Hill. |

THE DECISION

This is just the ending of a story — your answer in the exam would have several paragraphs building up to this point.

→ ... I knew I should never have stolen the vase. It had been a moment of madness. I had just seen it sitting there, and it looked so beautiful and elegant. All of my problems stemmed from that decision, that single flash of foolishness.

I spent a long time wondering what to do with the vase. I studied it intently. It was too beautiful to discard, too dazzling to keep concealed any longer. Eventually, I made a decision. I took it to the cliff and threw it over, watching it smash on the rocks below. It was an awful sight, but at least **my guilty secret**

You should build the tension towards a climax that will resolve the action.

After you've given a satisfying ending, you could go on to add an unexpected twist that leaves the reader with doubt in their mind.

→ **was gone forever.**

Late that night, the wind was howling around my tent, and the rain was pelting down on the canvas. Suddenly, there was a huge crash of thunder and a blinding flash of lightning. Terrified, I ran out of the tent, only to be greeted by a strange apparition: **there, sitting on top of a tree stump, was the missing vase. It was completely whole.** Not a single crack was visible on its smooth, shiny exterior. I whirled around and scoured the field for any sign of an intruder. **That was when I saw the old, hunched man walking slowly away.**

However you end your text, make sure it's exciting and powerful.

EXAM TIP

Your ending needs to be original and engaging...

You definitely shouldn't use clichéd endings like "it was all a dream" or "they all lived happily ever after" — the examiner wants to see that you have thought creatively about your answer.

Warm-Up Questions

Feeling chilly? No fear — these questions will get you feeling toasty in no time (when it comes to your English Language skills, that is). Use them as an introduction to the longer writing tasks on the next page.

Warm-Up Questions

1) Which of the following techniques are common in persuasive writing?
   a) an impersonal tone   b) rhetorical questions
   c) technical terms   d) emotive language

2) Rewrite the informative text below so that it persuades the reader to visit the church.

   ### Lyttlewich Church

   Situated in the rural village of Lyttlewich, Howtonshire, Lyttlewich Church is one of the oldest churches in the country: some parts of the church were built in 984 AD. The church receives thousands of visitors a year, and is particularly renowned for its artwork, which has recently been restored.

3) Rewrite each sentence below so that it's appropriate for an audience who have no expertise on the subject.
   a) Fertilisers provide phosphorous and potassium, which are essential for plant growth.
   b) The ossicle bones in the ear (the malleus, incus and stapes) are some of the smallest in the human skeleton.
   c) Roman legionaries used javelins and throwing-darts to defeat their enemies.

4) Write down a good opening sentence for each of the texts below.
   Make sure it's suitable for the audience given in the question.
   a) An article for a teenage magazine, in which you say that schools should spend more time teaching students how to manage their money.
   b) Instructions for a primary school student to teach them how to bake a cake.

5) Write a descriptive sentence about a busy leisure centre based on each of the following senses.
   a) sight   b) sound   c) touch   d) smell and/or taste

6) Write the closing sentences for each of the stories below.
   a) A story about a spaceship that crashes on an alien planet.
   b) A story set on a desert island.

7) Imagine you are going to write a short story about somebody who's lost in a forest.
   a) What narrative viewpoint would you use? Give a reason for your answer.
   b) Write down two descriptive adjectives you could use, and explain their effect.
   c) Write down a simile you could use.

8) You have been asked to write a story with the title 'The Castle'. Draw a spider diagram showing your ideas for things you might include.

Exam-Style Questions

These exam-style questions are like the question you'll find in section B of paper 1. It's a good idea to make a quick plan for your answers, because there are marks in this question for well-organised writing.

Q1

*In this question you will be assessed for the quality of your **creative prose writing** skills.*

Choose **one** of the following titles for your writing:

Either,	(a)	The Gang.
Or,	(b)	The Glass Staircase.
Or,	(c)	Write about your local area.
Or,	(d)	Write a story which begins: I should never have taken the long way home...

Q2

*In this question you will be assessed for the quality of your **creative prose writing** skills.*

Choose **one** of the following titles for your writing:

Either,	(a)	The Penguin.
Or,	(b)	Flying Home.
Or,	(c)	Write about a time when you went shopping.
Or,	(d)	Write a story which ends: ...I've never met anyone quite like her since.

Q3

*In this question you will be assessed for the quality of your **creative prose writing** skills.*

Choose **one** of the following titles for your writing:

Either,	(a)	Changing the World
Or,	(b)	The New Book
Or,	(c)	Write about a train journey.
Or,	(d)	Write a story which begins: There was simply no other option...

Writing Articles

Articles are non-fiction texts found in newspapers, magazines or on the Internet that are used to convey information, ideas or opinions to the reader. Have a look at the next three pages to find out more...

Articles **Report Events** and **Offer Opinions**

1) The main purpose of most articles is to <u>inform</u> people about <u>current affairs</u> or <u>other topics</u> of interest.

2) They do this in <u>two main ways</u>:

By directly reporting information	**By writing commentaries**
• Some articles are written to convey <u>facts</u> about a <u>story</u> or <u>theme</u>.	• Some articles are written to convey <u>facts</u> about a <u>story</u> or <u>theme</u>.
• They may report the viewpoints of <u>other people</u>, but the writer will not directly express their <u>own viewpoint</u> on the subject.	• They may report the viewpoints of <u>other people</u>, but the writer will not directly express their <u>own viewpoint</u> on the subject.
• The writer's <u>own viewpoint</u> might come across through the viewpoints of the people they <u>choose to quote</u>.	• The writer's <u>own viewpoint</u> might come across through the viewpoints of the people they <u>choose to quote</u>.

Articles need to **Engage** their **Audience**

1) If an article is <u>only</u> trying to convey facts, the writer will usually use an <u>unemotional tone</u>.

2) The register may be <u>technical</u> and the style quite <u>sophisticated</u>, in order to make the information seem <u>accurate</u> and <u>reliable</u>.

The author of the controversial report, Professor Hyde, has stated that, "agricultural reform is necessary to build a sustainable future". The report has, however, attracted widespread criticism from members of the agricultural community.		This conveys information in a <u>direct</u> way, using an <u>impersonal</u> tone, and with sophisticated, precise vocabulary. Viewpoints are conveyed by <u>quoting</u> and <u>paraphrasing</u>.

3) A commentary might use a <u>personal</u> tone and a <u>conversational</u> style to help convey the writer's <u>opinions</u> and <u>personality</u>.

It seems to me that this lot all need to take a deep breath and stop whinging. Nobody's going to bulldoze our green spaces any time soon — they'll have to spend 25 years making a planning application first.		This uses <u>colloquial</u> words to create a conversational style and <u>sarcasm</u> to convey the viewpoint of the writer.

4) <u>Rhetorical techniques</u> (see p.44) are commonly used in commentaries to help get the writer's opinions across forcefully and to encourage readers to <u>agree</u> with the writer.

What happened to the good old days, when the presence of a heap of spuds on the table at dinnertime brought delight all round? Has all this 'health food' nonsense made us forget our faithful starchy friend?		This uses <u>rhetorical questions</u> to engage and persuade the reader.

Writing Articles

The **Layout** of an article is **Important**

Articles often use <u>layout features</u> to engage the reader's <u>attention</u> and convey information <u>clearly</u>.

Headlines tell you, very briefly, what an article is about. Headlines need to capture the audience's interest so that they carry on reading the article. They might use techniques like alliteration or humour to achieve this.

Straplines are short statements that expand on the headline. They try to hook the reader further by giving more information about the story.

Subheadings are used to split an article up. Each subheading briefly tells you what the next section of text is about, often in an interesting or humorous way.

Articles often start with a short paragraph that gives an overview of the story or theme.

> ### SECRET WEDDING FOR DUTTON DUO
> **Private ceremony for TV's cutest couple**
>
> *By our showbiz reporter, Joe Snooping*
>
> Actors Simon Tremble and Katie Davies, stars of the TV series *Dutton Manor*, married yesterday at a secret ceremony in the Lake District.
>
> **LOVE AT FIRST SIGHT**
> According to insiders, the pair got together just three months ago and their engagement was only announced publicly last week. Thirty close friends and family, including several co-stars, joined them to celebrate, and pop sensation Al Blue performed at the reception.
>
> **DIRECTOR IS 'DELIGHTED'**
> Director of the series, Julian Parker, told The Daily Gossip that he was 'absolutely delighted' for the couple and added that they are 'perfect for each other'. However, he refused to comment on rumours that Simon's character in the show may be killed off when the new series begins in April.

Newspapers are aimed at a **General Audience**

1) A newspaper's main purpose is to <u>inform</u> people about <u>current affairs</u> and <u>other topics</u> that people are interested in.

2) Newspapers are mostly made up of informative <u>news reports</u>, although they also have <u>commentaries</u> that give the writer's <u>viewpoint</u> on a particular news story.

3) Most newspapers are aimed at a <u>wide</u>, <u>adult</u> audience, although they might <u>target</u> their articles towards a particular <u>political viewpoint</u> or <u>social class</u>.

> There are some exceptions to this, e.g. the audience for a school newspaper would be the students at the school.

4) Newspapers are broadly split into two types — <u>tabloids</u> and <u>broadsheets</u>.

- <u>Tabloids</u> (such as *The Sun* and *The Mirror*) tend to focus on more <u>sensational</u> topics and people, making their news stories accessible and with a wide appeal.

- <u>Broadsheets</u> (such as *The Telegraph* and *The Guardian*) are thought of as more <u>formal</u>, 'high-brow' journalism — focusing on what are thought to be more sophisticated topics.

Magazines are often about a **Special Interest**

1) <u>Magazines</u> usually focus on a particular <u>activity or interest</u>, such as fishing or art.

2) This means they need to appeal to their <u>particular audience</u>. This can be a <u>wide</u> audience, e.g. a magazine aimed at all women, or a more <u>specific</u> audience, e.g. a community magazine aimed at residents of a particular area.

> *I'd recommend some hardy perennials, such as peonies, which can provide a flash of much-needed colour during late spring and early summer.*

This text has a <u>specific</u> audience — it's aimed at people who are interested in <u>gardening</u>. It uses <u>specialist</u> language to convey the <u>writer's viewpoint</u> in an authoritative way.

3) Magazines tend to focus on <u>entertaining</u> the reader, so they will contain mostly <u>commentaries</u> — although some articles will be written purely to <u>inform</u> the reader.

Writing Articles

Internet Articles can be aimed at Any Audience

1) You might also be asked to write an article to be published <u>online</u>.
   This could be <u>either</u> a commentary <u>or</u> a news report.

2) Internet articles can have <u>any</u> purpose. This often depends on exactly <u>where</u> they're published
   — an article published on the website for a <u>broadsheet newspaper</u> could be purely <u>informative</u>,
   but an entry for a <u>blog</u> is likely to be written in a more <u>argumentative</u> way.

3) The audience for an online article might be <u>different</u> to that of traditional media,
   e.g. <u>younger</u> or with a different level of <u>understanding</u> about a subject.

4) Even though you're writing for an <u>online</u> audience, you should always
   use <u>Standard English</u> and avoid <u>abbreviations</u> or <u>smiley faces</u>.

Think about the Tone of your Article

PAPER 2

| 2 | 2 | You have a friend who claims that guided tours don't allow tourists to see the true heart of a country. You have decided to write an article for a travel magazine to share your views on this idea. You could agree or disagree with their opinion. **Write a lively article for the magazine giving your views.** |

This question is asking you to give your opinion on a topic.

Use a strapline to summarise the article in an interesting way.

FORGET THE ROAD LESS TRAVELLED

Guided tours are the best way to experience somewhere new.

Your headline needs to be short and punchy to engage the reader.

You're giving an opinion, so your tone should be quite personal.

At some point or other, we've all encountered a travel snob: that particular breed of traveller who knows all about where to go, what to see and, most importantly, how to see it. The travel snob thinks that guided tours are for the uncultured bores. The travel snob believes in travel without a destination. And yet, the travel snob will always find time to tell you about a 'hidden gem' that only they can take you to.

Use rhetorical devices like repetition to make your writing entertaining.

You would think someone so worldly-wise would see the irony by now — travel snobs are themselves tour guides. Their cherished 'off the beaten track' spots are transported, by their own recommendation, right onto 'the beaten track' — they're the ones beating it, leading the tourists away from well-known honeypot sites and into 'the heart of things'.

You can use a sarcastic tone to give your writing a sense of personality.

Opinion articles often combine a conversational style with complex sentences and vocabulary.

In the meantime, guided tours are often run by local people, who will frequently have a real treasure trove of local knowledge. How can a throwaway recommendation from an outsider possibly surpass that? Anybody who wants to see the true heart of a country must be guided by the people who live in it.

Make sure you link your answer to the prompt you're given in the question.

It's a good idea to read some real-life articles...

While revising, it's worth looking at some real articles from different sources. You'll start to spot patterns in the vocabulary and structure that they use, which will help you write a good answer.

Writing Leaflets

Leaflets need to give the reader lots of information in a clear, organised way.

Leaflets can have **Varied Audiences** and **Purposes**

1) Leaflets can have <u>any</u> purpose, but they're often used to <u>advise</u> (e.g. a leaflet advising the reader to open a savings account) or <u>persuade</u> an audience (e.g. to vote for a particular political party).

2) They can have a <u>general audience</u> (e.g. a leaflet about the importance of healthy eating) or a more <u>specific audience</u> (e.g. a leaflet advertising a particular museum or exhibition).

3) Leaflets need a <u>clear structure</u> to <u>break up</u> information. This could include:

> • a clear title   • subheadings   • bullet points

4) Leaflets also need to <u>grab the reader's attention</u>, so that they <u>remember</u> all the information they're given. You can use <u>language techniques</u>, such as <u>lists of three</u> or <u>direct address</u>, to achieve this.

Organise your **Leaflet** in a **Clear** and **Interesting** way

> PAPER 2

> | 2 | 1 |
>
> Your local pet shelter is struggling with the number of animals they have to look after.
>
> **Write the text for a leaflet aimed at people in your local area, in which you persuade them to adopt a pet from the local pet shelter.**
>
> You could include:
>
> • examples of the types of pet they can adopt;
> • reasons to go to the local pet shelter instead of elsewhere.

Use a title to catch the attention of the target audience (people who might want to adopt a pet).

→ THINKING OF GETTING A PET?

This addresses the reader in a direct, flattering way, which creates a personal connection that makes the reader more likely to trust the writer.

You'll probably have considered the type of pet you want to get, and how you'll find the time to feed and care for it — but have you considered where you'll adopt your pet from?

Use subheadings to organise your answer and summarise your points clearly.

<u>Shelters — the sensible option</u>

Most people go straight to a local pet shop without thinking, but it's definitely worth checking pet shelters first. Lots of the animals there have been left homeless through no fault of their own, and they're often friendly and affectionate — and house-trained!

<u>Your local shelter needs you</u>

Tinsby Pet Shelter is a small, charity-funded organisation that cares for abandoned and homeless pets in Tinsby and the surrounding area. We currently look after:

Short paragraphs can help to break up the information in a text.

| • | Dogs | • | Rabbits | • | Guinea Pigs | • | Reptiles |
| • | Cats | • | Hamsters | • | Birds | • | ... and even a frog or two! |

Bullet points are used to show that there are lots of different animals available for adoption.

Unfortunately, many of these adorable animals will never find a new home. And whilst we do our best to keep them happy and healthy, it's no substitute for a loving full-time owner. So don't wait — visit us today. **Your new pet can't wait to meet you!** ←

This emotive sentence persuades the reader by appealing to their feelings.

 EXAM TIP

You should think about who is reading your leaflet...

Leaflets can be written for a variety of different audiences. Make sure your leaflet is adapted to the audience you're given by choosing a suitable writing style that uses appropriate language.

Travel Writing

Travel writing needs to effectively convey your feelings about the place you're writing about.

Travel Writing is **Personal** and **Informal**

1) Travel writing is an <u>account</u> of a writer's travels to a specific <u>place</u>.

2) If you're asked to produce some travel writing, you'll need to convey your <u>thoughts</u> and <u>opinions</u> about the place you're writing about, as well as give some <u>information</u> about it.

3) A piece of travel writing can <u>entertain</u> the reader (e.g. if it's in a book or magazine), <u>inform</u> them (e.g. if it's in a travel guide), or <u>persuade</u> them to visit a destination.

4) However, it's usually written for a <u>combination</u> of these purposes, e.g. <u>travel guides</u> are often written to both <u>inform</u> and <u>entertain</u> the reader.

5) Travel writing usually has an <u>informal</u> register and a <u>chatty</u> style, and it's almost always written in the <u>first person</u>. Try to write as if you're having a <u>conversation</u> with the audience, but don't forget to use lots of <u>descriptive techniques</u> too.

Use **Interesting Language** to **Convey** your **Opinions**

PAPER 2

| 2 | 2 |
You have decided to write an article for a national travel magazine to share your views about a destination you have visited. You could write in favour or against visiting the destination.
Write an entertaining article for the magazine giving your views.

This question asks you to write a magazine article. It needs to be entertaining and informative, and could also persuade the reader to agree with your point of view.

An interesting, punchy title and strapline can help to grab your audience's attention.

Dismayed in Manhattan

Lucy Farthing says "no thanks" to New York.

I've travelled to many cities during my career as a travel writer, and it's fair to say that there are a few I'd rather have avoided. **None, however, have quite matched up to the discomfort and sheer frustration I experienced in New York.**

Use personal pronouns like 'I' to make the tone of your writing more personal.

I suspect my high expectations didn't help. Before embarking on my trip, I'd been regaled with stories from friends and family who'd already visited the place. "It's the city of dreams", I was told; "the best city in the world!"

Make your opinion on the destination very clear.

What I realised instead, somewhere between my fifth cup of overpriced coffee and my fourteenth hour-long queue, was that **New York is the city of nightmares**. Not only did it feel like the world's busiest city, it felt like the **noisiest**, too; by the end of my week there I found myself longing for the joys of silence and solitude. Maybe for some, New York is a city where dreams come true, but it was certainly far from the **inspiring haven** I had hoped to find.

Try to use all five senses to create a sense of the atmosphere of the place.

Use interesting language to make your text more entertaining.

Practise using descriptive language in your travel writing...

Imagine you are a travel writer and have been asked to write an article about your favourite place or country. For each of the five senses, write a sentence describing the place you have chosen.

Writing Reports and Essays

Reports and essays use a similar tone and style, but they do have one difference — their typical audience.

Reports and Essays are Similar

1) Reports and essays should be <u>impersonal</u> and <u>objective</u> in tone. You'll need to go through the arguments <u>for</u> and <u>against</u> something, then come to a conclusion that demonstrates your <u>own point of view</u>.

2) Reports and essays should follow a <u>logical structure</u>. They need to have:

- An <u>introduction</u> that sets up the <u>main theme</u>.
- Well-structured <u>paragraphs</u> covering the <u>strengths</u> and <u>weaknesses</u> of the arguments.
- A <u>conclusion</u> that ties things together and offers <u>your own</u> point of view.

3) The purpose of reports and essays is almost always to <u>inform</u>, but they often <u>advise</u> their audience too.

4) You need to make sure you write for the correct <u>audience</u> — <u>essays</u> usually have quite a <u>general</u> audience, but <u>reports</u> are normally written for a <u>particular</u> person or group of people.

Reports should Analyse and Advise

2 1   Your school has received a grant to fund extra-curricular activities.
Write a report for the board of governors suggesting how they could spend the money.
You could include:
- examples of extra-curricular activities they could spend the money on;
- your ideas about how the money might best be spent.

At the start, show that you are clearly aware of who your audience is.

You don't need to create any suspense — give your opinion in the introduction.

Phrases like 'on the one hand' show that you have thought about both sides of the argument.

<u>A Report Into The Possible Uses Of The Extra-Curricular Budget</u>

This report has been commissioned by the board of governors to identify the best use of the funds available for extra-curricular activities at St. Swithins Park Secondary School. Two options have been investigated: the rock-climbing club and the film society. After careful consideration of the evidence collected from various interviews and data analysis, **the conclusion has been reached that the film club is the most logical recipient of the funds.**

On the one hand, the rock-climbing club appears to be the most obvious choice as it is the most costly to run: the club organises frequent expeditions involving expensive equipment and high travel costs. Having said that, the club does charge a members' fee, which helps to alleviate some of this financial burden.

Your language should be very formal and impersonal, but you still need to convey a viewpoint.

In the real answer, you would go on to include several more paragraphs and finish with a conclusion that gives advice.

Your reports and essays should have an impersonal tone...

Reports and essays are quite simple to write — just make sure that you're being as objective, analytical and formal as possible. But you must make sure that you still show a viewpoint by coming to a conclusion.

Writing Reviews

People read reviews to find out the writer's opinion about something, so you need to express yours clearly.

Reviews should **Entertain** as well as **Inform**

1) A <u>review</u> is a piece of writing that gives an <u>opinion</u> about how <u>good</u> something is — it might be a book, a piece of music or even an exhibition.

2) <u>Reviews</u> can appear in lots of <u>different</u> publications. If you have to write a review in the exam, the question will usually tell you <u>where</u> it's going to appear.

3) The <u>publication</u> where your review appears will affect what kind of <u>audience</u> you're writing for and <u>how</u> you write. For example, a film review for a teen magazine could be <u>funny</u> and <u>chatty</u>, but a review of a Shakespeare play for a broadsheet newspaper should be <u>serious</u> and <u>informative</u>.

4) You should also pay attention to <u>purpose</u>. Your review could have <u>several</u> different purposes:

- Your review needs to <u>entertain</u> the reader.
- You also need to <u>inform</u> the reader about the thing you're reviewing, based on your <u>own opinion</u>.
- You might also need to <u>advise</u> the reader whether or not to see or do the thing you're reviewing.

5) <u>Don't</u> get too hung up on <u>describing</u> everything in minute detail — it's much more important to give your <u>opinion</u>, and keep your review <u>engaging</u> by focusing on the <u>interesting bits</u> and using <u>sophisticated language</u>.

Your review needs to **Give** an **Evaluation**

PAPER 2

| 2 2 | Imagine you have been to a music concert.
You have decided to write a review for a broadsheet newspaper to share your views about the concert. You could write about it in a positive or negative way.
Write a review for the newspaper giving your views. |

This review is for a broadsheet newspaper, so make sure you adapt your writing appropriately — use a formal register with fairly complex language.

'Music through the Millennium': A Feast for the Ears

Make your opinion clear from the start of the review.

Make sure your review is informative as well as entertaining.

From the moment the audience took their seats, the auditorium was buzzing with excitement, **and they were not to be disappointed**. This stunning collection of **classical and contemporary pieces** took the audience on an unforgettable journey through **a thousand years of music**, from the intense gloom and misery of funeral marches to the pounding excitement of percussion movements, and the intense joy of some truly superb symphonies. This was a sonic experience not to be missed: a congregation of musical heavyweights that each **packed a punch strong enough to knock the emotional stuffing out of even the stoniest of hearts**. From start to end, 'Music through the Millennium' was a true schooling in the stirring power of music.

Use figurative language to make your review interesting.

Think about how you might review films or music...

When you're listening to music or watching a film, think about what you might write if you were asked to write a review for it. Think about the things you liked/disliked and your overall opinion.

Writing Speeches

A speech needs to be powerful and moving. You should aim to have an emotional effect on your audience.

Speeches need to be Dramatic and Engaging

1) Speeches are often written to argue or persuade, so they need to have a dramatic, emotional impact on their audience.

2) One way to make a speech persuasive is to give it an effective structure — arrange your points so that they build tension throughout your answer, then end with an emotive or exciting climax.

3) You can use lots of language techniques to make your writing engaging and persuasive:

> *These accusations are hateful, hurtful and humiliating.* → Alliteration and the use of a list of three adjectives make this sound strong and angry.

Persuasive language techniques like these are known as rhetorical devices — see page 44.

> *Do we really have no other option? The current situation is a disgrace!* → Rhetorical questions and exclamations engage the reader and make your writing sound more like spoken language.

4) Remember that speeches are spoken, not read. Try to use techniques that are effective when they're spoken out loud.

Your speech should Make People Think

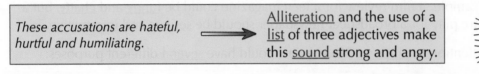

PAPER 2

| 2 2 | A proposal has been made to build a new zoo in your local area. You have decided to make a speech at a local community meeting to share your views on this proposal. You could argue in favour or against this proposal. **Write an engaging speech giving your views.** |

Try to use lots of personal pronouns like 'I', 'you' and 'we' to engage your audience.

The word 'must' creates a confident tone.

You could use repetition to increase the dramatic impact of your speech.

Ladies and gentlemen, I am here today to defend the proposal to build a new zoo in Upper Babbleton. I believe that a zoo would be hugely beneficial to our local community.

Modern British zoos are primarily focused on conservation and education. To my mind, these are important values. We **must** impress upon the young people of Upper Babbleton the need to protect endangered species and habitats. **A zoo can help us to do this.** Modern zoos offer extensive opportunities for these kinds of educational experiences: there are interactive exhibitions, talks from conservationists and live question-and-answer forums that will help to educate our young people.

The new zoo will help us inspire a generation with the importance of conservation. **It will help us** raise awareness of environmental issues. **It will help us** by providing a space in which we can work together to build a **safer, greener and more ecologically friendly world.**

Start off by addressing your listeners directly and announcing the reason for your speech — show that you've understood your purpose and audience.

Vary the lengths of your sentences to show pauses and emphasis.

Use rhetorical devices like lists of three to make your argument sound more forceful.

REVISION TASK

Look at famous speeches for inspiration...

There are plenty of famous speeches throughout history — find a few that you find interesting and make a note of the techniques they use. You could then try to use these techniques in your writing.

Writing Letters

Letters are always addressed to a particular person or group of people. This means that they have very specific audiences, so it's very important that you tailor your letter to suit that audience.

Letters can be Formal or Informal

1) If you're asked to write a <u>letter</u>, look at the <u>audience</u> to see if you need to use a <u>formal</u> or <u>informal</u> register.

2) If the letter is to someone you <u>don't</u> know well, or to someone in a position of <u>authority</u>, keep it <u>formal</u> with a <u>serious</u> tone. This means you should:

   - Use <u>formal greetings</u> (e.g. 'Dear Sir/Madam') and <u>sign-offs</u> (e.g. 'Yours sincerely' if you've used their name, 'Yours faithfully' if you haven't).

   - Use <u>Standard English</u> and <u>formal vocabulary</u>, e.g. you could use phrases like 'In my opinion...' or 'I find this state of affairs...'.

3) If the letter is to a <u>friend</u> or <u>relative</u>, or someone your <u>own</u> age, you should use a more <u>informal</u> register and <u>personal</u> tone. This means you should:

   - Start with your reader's <u>name</u>, e.g. 'Dear Jenny', and <u>sign off</u> with 'best wishes' or 'warm regards'.

   - Make sure you still write in <u>Standard English</u> (so no <u>text speak</u> or <u>slang</u>) and show the examiner that you can use interesting <u>vocabulary</u> and <u>sentence structures</u>.

Don't make your Letter too Chatty

PAPER 2

> | 2 | 2 | This is part of an article that appeared in a newspaper:
>
> 'International travel is not worth the cost when there are much cheaper alternatives closer to home. Holidays in the UK cost significantly less and offer the same benefits as a holiday abroad.'
>
> You have decided to write a letter to the newspaper to explain your point of view. You could write in favour or against international travel.
>
> **Write a letter to the newspaper giving your views.**

This letter is for somebody in a position of authority, so it uses a formal greeting.

You need to make your viewpoint clear.

Dear Sir or Madam,

    I read with dismay your recent article regarding international travel. As a regular traveller myself, **I strongly disagree with your assertion that international travel is not worth the cost.** The benefits of international travel far outweigh the expenses incurred: it broadens the mind, adds to your wealth of experience and heightens your awareness of the world around you.

    The article claims that **UK holidays are cheaper and provide similar benefits.** If you are not deterred by the threat of drizzle, perhaps that is true. To me, however, it is worth spending a fraction more to avoid wasting your holidays sheltering from the British rain.

Formal language like this helps to set the right tone for your letter and shows that you've understood your audience.

Introducing a counter-argument, then contradicting it, can help to build up your argument.

You need to write for your audience, but keep your writing high-level...

You will need to pay attention to purpose and audience — make sure your letter completes the task in the question and is written in an appropriate style. Whoever your audience is, you always need to write well.

Worked Answer

Before you leave this section, have a look at this worked answer for paper 2.

| 2 | 2 |

This is part of a speech you recently heard:

"In order to prepare young adults for the challenges of raising a family, it should be made compulsory for them to spend time volunteering with young children."

Write an article for a broadsheet newspaper giving your views on this subject.

When you're planning, it might help to jot down all your <u>ideas</u> first, and then <u>organise</u> them afterwards.

<u>PLAN</u>

own experience at nursery in Y10 — negative — put off having children. Cover some counter-arguments. My arguments = time pressure on young people; not all want to become parents; natural anyway? Where do you find all the children/parental permission etc.

- Para 1: own experience at nursery in Y10

- Para 2: Counter-arguments: skills (selflessness, communication, imagination), responsibility, prep for parenthood

- Para 3: not all want to become parents (figure?); those who do will be fine (natural process)

- Para 4: time pressure on young people as it is — studying, home life, part-time job already perhaps, already pressured enough into thinking of future

- Para 5: logistical problems (finding the children; those children's parents' views on it; how/who/what)

- Para 6: conclusion — well done to those doing it, sure it's rewarding, but shouldn't be compulsory

Make sure you know what your overall <u>opinion</u> is <u>before</u> you start writing.

It's great to use interesting language techniques, like <u>similes</u>, to help your reader to <u>empathise</u> with you.

DON'T PUSH TEENS INTO PARENTING PRACTICE

When I was fifteen, my school Careers Advisor decided that the best way to teach her Year Tens about the wonderful ways of life was to dump them into the world of work. And so, <u>like a bemused traveller without a map</u>, I found myself, dazed and confused, in my local preschool. I have nothing against this preschool in particular, but the week I spent there was one of the most unpleasant of my life. After the fourth day of being smeared with paint, wet sand and the bodily fluids of various toddlers, I swore I would never work with children again. <u>Which is why I find it remarkable that there are proposals to make this experience compulsory.</u>

Using an <u>anecdote</u> provides an <u>engaging</u> opening.

The <u>descriptive language</u> in this sentence helps the reader to imagine the scene at the preschool.

Your <u>opinion</u> on the statement needs to be <u>clear</u> — even if you don't state it explicitly like this.

It is true that there are several strong arguments in favour of making volunteering with young children compulsory for young adults. It would teach them the patience, selflessness and imaginative thinking necessary for raising a child — important lessons for future parenthood. Furthermore, after first-hand exposure to young

Show that you're responding to the <u>prompt</u> in the question.

Worked Answer

The second paragraph is <u>slightly inappropriate</u> for the <u>form</u> — it's become a bit like an essay. It would be better if the <u>style</u> was <u>less formal</u>...

children, other young adults may decide that parenthood would not suit them at all, and be able to make more informed choices later in life.

However, I struggle to comprehend how any young adult could actually finish their compulsory volunteering thinking "yes please". The lessons I was taught at the preschool included "there is no such thing as a clean child" and "home time is the only time worth treasuring". <u>It's also worth remembering</u> that some young people already have no intention of becoming parents. In a recent survey, <u>10%</u> of them said they had no desire to have children. I would like to see how many of the other 90% flock to join them after an <u>enforced week of torture</u> such as mine.

...like this. This kind of <u>informal phrase</u> is better suited to a broadsheet newspaper article.

<u>Facts and figures</u> are <u>appropriate</u> for a broadsheet newspaper article.

<u>Hyperbole</u> can be used to add <u>humour</u>, making your answer <u>entertaining</u>.

This is before we even consider that many young people simply wouldn't have the time for volunteering. My own week of work experience meant losing a week of lessons while studying for my GCSEs. Plenty of young people are already ground to the bone, juggling <u>home life, academics and extra-curricular activities</u> in the hope of getting that important first job. <u>Surely this should take priority over spending stressful time with children?</u>

Rhetorical techniques (like <u>rhetorical questions</u> and <u>lists of three</u>) make your answer more <u>persuasive</u>.

Broadsheet newspaper articles should have a <u>personal tone</u>.

Where these children would come from is another mystery. <u>Personally</u>, I can't imagine my own parents willingly donating me for an unknown teenager to take care of. I also feel sorry for whichever local schools, preschools or councils would become responsible for dealing with the <u>mountains of paperwork</u> involved.

This <u>metaphor</u> adds <u>emphasis</u> to the point about logistical problems.

This conclusion refers back to the <u>statement</u> in the question, which links the answer together nicely, and shows good <u>organisation</u>.

In theory, bringing young people and young children together for voluntary work seems like a lovely idea. I'm sure there are plenty of young people who already volunteer with young children, and I'm sure they benefit from it. This does not mean that we should start forcing all of their peers into it too — a few hours with a messy, crying child isn't going to prepare you <u>for the challenges of raising a family</u>, because you're never going to want to have a family at all.

- This answer is mostly well-matched to its form (a broadsheet newspaper article), and shows a good awareness of purpose (to persuade and entertain) and audience (readers of a broadsheet newspaper).

- It also uses a variety of language techniques effectively (e.g. similes, hyperbole and rhetorical questions).

- The structure is good too. It's written in clear paragraphs, with an engaging introduction and conclusion.

- To get the very top marks, this answer could use some more ambitious vocabulary and punctuation. The second paragraph would also need to be better-matched to the form in the question.

Exam-Style Questions

These questions will help you to prepare for the writing questions in paper 2. Make sure you quickly plan your answers — in the real exam, there are marks for a well-organised response to each question.

Q1

Your local community leaders are concerned that active hobbies, such as sports, are falling by the wayside in favour of time spent using tablets or smartphones.

Write an article for your local newspaper advising people how to spend less time in front of screens and more time engaging in active hobbies.

You could include:
- ideas for how to cut down on the use of tablets or smartphones;
- examples of active hobbies to get involved in.

Q2

One of your classmates has said that going to bed early is a waste of time, as all worthwhile television programmes are on late at night.

You have decided to write a speech to persuade your class to agree with your views on this idea. You could write for or against the idea.

Write a compelling speech giving your views.

Q3

You have read a leaflet for a tour company which says young people should travel and experience new cultures before they start their adult life.

You have decided to write a piece of travel writing for a broadsheet newspaper in which you share your views on this idea. You could write in favour or against this idea.

Write an entertaining piece of travel writing giving your views.

Q4

This is part of an article that appeared in a local newspaper:

"We should build more houses in rural areas. Having beautiful scenery is not as important as having a plentiful supply of housing for a growing population."

You have decided to write a letter to the editor of the newspaper to share your views on this subject. You could write in favour or against this statement.

Write a compelling letter giving your views.

Revision Summary

This is the final Revision Summary in this book (hurrah) so make sure you use it well.

- Try these questions and <u>tick off each one</u> when you <u>get it right</u>.
- When you've done <u>all the questions</u> under a heading and are <u>completely happy</u> with it, tick it off.

Writing with Purpose (p.62-68) ☑

1) What would be the purpose of an answer to this question?
   Write the opening of a short story about a lost pet.

2) True or false?
   *You never have to work out the audience in a writing question
   — it will be stated for you explicitly every time.*

3) Why might an advert for children's breakfast cereal have more than one audience?

4) What three things do you always need to match to your purpose and audience?

5) Give two ways in which you could start a story so that it's engaging for the reader.

6) Rewrite this sentence so that it has a first-person narrative viewpoint.
   Frances skulked down the hallway, delaying her arrival at her Maths classroom.

7) Give one effect of using a third-person narrative viewpoint.

8) Which of these would be a good way to end a story?
   a) A question that creates a cliffhanger.
   b) An unexpected plot twist to shock the reader.
   c) And they all lived happily ever after.

Writing in Different Styles (p.71-79) ☑

9) Give two ways that articles inform people.

10) Give three layout features that you could include in an article.

11) What is a broadsheet newspaper?

12) Give an example of a specific audience a magazine article might be aimed at.

13) How might an article written for a blog be different to an article published
    on the website of a broadsheet newspaper?

14) Name two structural features that you could use to break up information in a leaflet.

15) What would be the form and purpose, and who would be the audience, in an answer to this
    exam question?
    *This is part of an article you have read:
    "Holidays to Europe are overrated — today's European cities are busy, expensive and dull."
    Imagine you have just visited a city in Europe. Write an article for a travel magazine
    giving your views on this subject.*

16) Briefly explain the logical structure you should use when writing a report or an essay.

17) What is the main difference between a report and an essay?

18) How should your style of writing be different in a game review for a teen magazine,
    and an album review for a broadsheet newspaper?

19) What is usually your main purpose when you're writing a speech?

20) Write down an example opening and ending for:
    a) a letter to a local councillor, arguing in favour of building a new shopping centre near
       where you live
    b) a letter to a named teacher, asking for an extension on your homework deadline.

Sample Exam — Paper 1

These two pages show you some example questions that are like the ones you'll see in paper 1 — the source to go with the questions in section A is on pages 86-87. First, have a read through the questions and the source, then have a look at the handy graded answer extracts we've provided on pages 87-97.

Section A — Reading

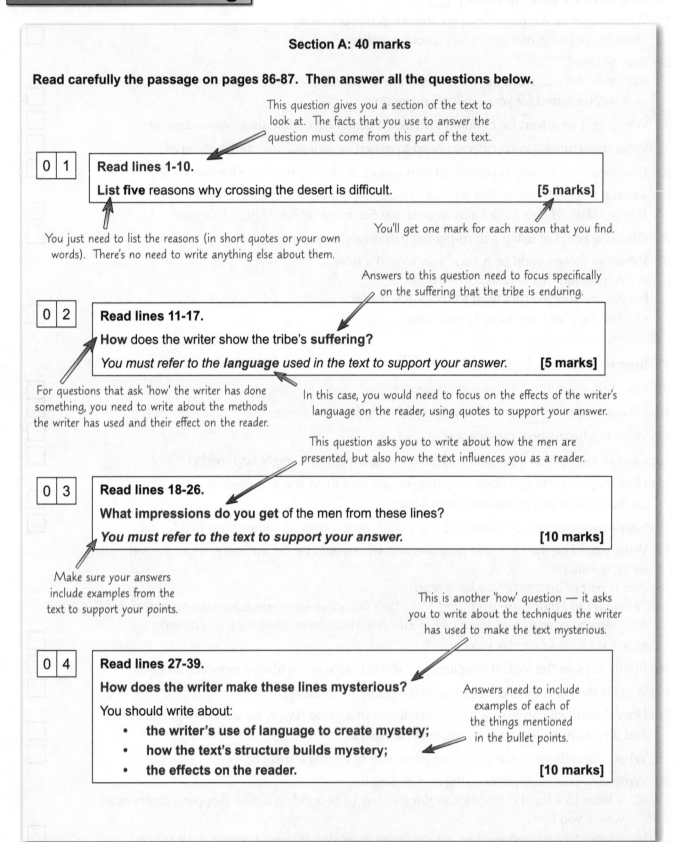

Section A: 40 marks

Read carefully the passage on pages 86-87. Then answer all the questions below.

This question gives you a section of the text to look at. The facts that you use to answer the question must come from this part of the text.

0	1

Read lines 1-10.

List five reasons why crossing the desert is difficult.   **[5 marks]**

You just need to list the reasons (in short quotes or your own words). There's no need to write anything else about them.

You'll get one mark for each reason that you find.

Answers to this question need to focus specifically on the suffering that the tribe is enduring.

0	2

Read lines 11-17.

How does the writer show the tribe's suffering?

You must refer to the language used in the text to support your answer.   **[5 marks]**

For questions that ask 'how' the writer has done something, you need to write about the methods the writer has used and their effect on the reader.

In this case, you would need to focus on the effects of the writer's language on the reader, using quotes to support your answer.

This question asks you to write about how the men are presented, but also how the text influences you as a reader.

0	3

Read lines 18-26.

What impressions do you get of the men from these lines?

You must refer to the text to support your answer.   **[10 marks]**

Make sure your answers include examples from the text to support your points.

This is another 'how' question — it asks you to write about the techniques the writer has used to make the text mysterious.

0	4

Read lines 27-39.

How does the writer make these lines mysterious?

You should write about:
- **the writer's use of language to create mystery;**
- **how the text's structure builds mystery;**
- **the effects on the reader.**   **[10 marks]**

Answers need to include examples of each of the things mentioned in the bullet points.

Sample Exam — Paper 1

This question is a bit different — it asks you to write about a specific part of the text and the text as a whole.

| 0 | 5 | **Read lines 40 to the end.** |

"In the last two paragraphs of this passage, the writer encourages the reader to feel sympathy for the tribe."

To what extent do you agree with this view? ← *Evaluate the text by explaining how much you agree with the statement.*

You should write about:

- **your own impressions of the tribe** and its surroundings, **both here and in the passage as a whole;**

- **how** the writer has created these impressions.

You must refer to the text to support your answer. **[10 marks]**

You need to write about your own opinion of the text and the methods the writer has used to make you feel like this.

You should always include plenty of evidence from the text in your answers.

Section B — Writing

You will need to write a piece of prose fiction for this question — so don't write a piece of poetry or a play.

Section B: 40 marks

*In this section, you will be assessed for the quality of your **creative prose writing** skills.*

24 marks are awarded for communication and organisation.
16 marks are awarded for vocabulary, sentence structure, spelling and punctuation.

You should aim to write about 450-600 words.

You're given four options, but you only need to pick one of them.

For writing questions, you get marks for how you write (i.e. the language and structure you use) and the accuracy of your writing (i.e. your spelling, punctuation and grammar).

| 1 | 1 | **Choose one of the following titles for your writing:** |

Either, *(a)* Taking a Chance

Or, *(b)* The Cabin

Or, *(c)* Write about a time when you were at a theme park.

Or, *(d)* Write a story which ends:
"…We never discussed the mysterious events of that night again." **[40 marks]**

The answers to these questions are in the rest of the section...

You don't have to answer these questions yourself. Instead, read on for some sample answers, which will give you an idea of what you need to write in your exam. You can refer back to these pages if you need to.

Literature Extract

Here's the text to go with the questions on pages 84-85. It's an extract from the opening of the novel *Desert*, by J.M.G. Le Clézio, which was published in 1980. The extract describes a tribe's journey across a desert.

They walked noiselessly in the sand, slowly, not watching where they were going. The wind blew relentlessly, the desert wind, hot in the daytime, cold at night. The sand swirled about them, between the legs of the camels, lashing the faces of the women, who pulled the blue veils down over their eyes. The young children ran about, the babies cried, rolled up in the blue cloth on their mothers' backs. The
5 camels growled, sneezed. No one knew where the caravan was going.

The sun was still high in the stark sky, sounds and smells were swept away on the wind. Sweat trickled slowly down the faces of the travelers; the dark skin on their cheeks, on their arms and legs was tinted with indigo. The blue tattoos on the women's foreheads looked like shiny little beetles. Their black eyes, like drops of molten metal, hardly seeing the immense stretch of sand, searched for signs of the trail in
10 the rolling dunes.

There was nothing else on earth, nothing, no one. They were born of the desert, they could follow no other path. They said nothing. Wanted nothing. The wind swept over them, through them, as if there were no one on the dunes. They had been walking since the very crack of dawn without stopping, thirst and weariness hung over them like a lead weight. Their cracked lips and tongues were
15 hard and leathery. Hunger gnawed their insides. They couldn't have spoken. They had been as mute as the desert for so long, filled with the light of the sun burning down in the middle of the empty sky, and frozen with the night and its still stars.

They continued to make their slow way down the slope toward the valley bottom, zigzagging when loose sand shifted out from under their feet. The men chose where their feet would come down without
20 looking. It was as if they were walking along invisible trails leading them out to the other end of solitude, to the night. Only one of them carried a gun, a flintlock rifle with a long barrel of blackened copper. He carried it on his chest, both arms folded tightly over it, the barrel pointing upward like a flagpole. His brothers walked alongside him, wrapped in their cloaks, bending slightly forward under the weight of their burdens. Beneath their cloaks, the blue clothing was in tatters, torn by thorns, worn by the sand.
25 Behind the weary herd, Nour, the son of the man with the rifle, walked in front of his mother and sisters. His face was dark, sun-scorched, but his eyes shone and the light of his gaze was almost supernatural.

They were the men and the women of the sand, of the wind, of the light, of the night. They had appeared as if in a dream at the top of a dune, as if they were born of the cloudless sky and carried the harshness of space in their limbs. They bore with them hunger, the thirst of bleeding lips, the flintlike
30 silence of the glinting sun, the cold nights, the glow of the Milky Way, the moon; accompanying them were their huge shadows at sunset, the waves of virgin sand over which their splayed feet trod, the inaccessible horizon. More than anything, they bore the light of their gaze shining so brightly in the whites of their eyes.

The herd of grayish-brown goats and sheep walked in front of the children. The beasts also moved
35 forward not knowing where, their hooves following in ancient tracks. The sand whirled between their legs, stuck in their dirty coats. One man led the dromedaries* simply with his voice, grumbling and spitting as they did. The hoarse sound of labored breathing caught in the wind, then suddenly disappeared in the hollows of the dunes to the south. But the wind, the dryness, the hunger, no longer mattered. The people and the herd moved slowly down toward the waterless, shadeless valley bottom.

40 They'd been walking like that for months, years maybe. They'd followed the routes of the sky between the waves of sand, the routes coming from the Drâa**, from Tamgrout, from the Erg Iguidi, or farther north — the route of the Aït Atta, of the Gheris, coming from Tafilelt, that joins the great *ksours*** in the foothills of the Atlas Mountains, or else the endless route that penetrates into the heart of the desert, beyond Hank, in the direction of the great city of Timbuktu. Some died along the way, others were born,
45 were married. Animals died too, throats slit open to fertilize the entrails of the earth, or else stricken with the plague and left to rot on the hard ground.

It was as if there were no names here, as if there were no words. The desert cleansed everything in its wind, wiped everything away. The men had the freedom of the open spaces in their eyes, their

Graded Answers — Section A, Question 1

> 50 | skin was like metal. Sunlight blazed everywhere. The ochre, yellow, gray, white sand, the fine sand shifted, showing the direction of the wind. It covered all traces, all bones. It repelled light, drove away water, life, far from a center that no one could recognize. The men knew perfectly well that the desert wanted nothing to do with them: so they walked on without stopping, following the paths that other feet had already traveled in search of something else. As for water, it was in the *aiun*: the eyes that were the color of the sky, or else in the damp beds of old muddy streams. But it wasn't water for pleasure
> 55 | or for refreshment either. It was just a sweat mark on the surface of the desert, the meager gift of an arid God, the last shudder of life. Heavy water wrenched from the sand, dead water from crevices, alkaline water that caused colic, vomiting. They must walk even farther, bending slightly forward, in the direction the stars had indicated.
>
> **Glossary**
> *   dromedaries — camels
> **   Drâa, Tamgrout, Erg Iguidi, Aït Atta, Gheris, Tafilelt — places, regions and tribes of North Africa
> *** *ksours* — fortified villages

Now that you've had a chance to look at the questions and the text, the next few pages have some sample answers for you to look at.

Here's a reminder of the **First Question**

0	1	**Read lines 1-10.**
		List **five** reasons why crossing the desert is difficult. **[5 marks]**

Check your **Facts Carefully**

The facts you pick out can either be explicit or implicit (see p.12 for more on this)

1) The first question in section A asks for <u>five</u> reasons why crossing the desert is difficult. You get <u>one</u> mark for <u>each</u> correct reason you write down.

2) There's no need to <u>analyse</u> the facts — the examiner wants you to <u>find</u> information from the text.

3) Careful though — all the facts should come from <u>lines 1-10</u>. It's also important to <u>check</u> every fact carefully — anything that's <u>inaccurate</u> or doesn't refer to why crossing the desert is <u>difficult</u> won't get a mark.

4) You can lose marks if you use quotes that are too <u>long</u>, so don't just copy out <u>whole sentences</u>.

This is a **Grade 4-5** answer

You should be aiming for full marks on this question if you're after grades 8-9.

This answer is correct, so it would get a mark.

1 → The wind was blowing "relentlessly".

2   They have to search for the trail in the sand. ◄

3   The sun and the wind are hot in the daytime. ◄

This quote is too long, so it's not clear what exactly is being referred to. This answer wouldn't get a mark.

4   "The camels growled". ◄

5   "The sun was still high in the stark sky, sounds and smells were swept away on the wind."

For question 1, it's fine to paraphrase instead of directly quoting — these answers would also get marks.

The camels growling isn't a reason for the desert crossing being difficult, so it wouldn't get a mark.

Graded Answers — Section A, Question 2

The second question in section A is trickier. Look at these sample answers for advice on how to answer it.

Here's the **Second Question** again

> **0 2** **Read lines 11-17.**
>
> How does the writer show the tribe's suffering?
>
> *You must refer to the language used in the text to support your answer.*   **[5 marks]**

Pick out key **Language Features** and **Explain** their **Effects**

1) The second question in section A tests how well you can explain the effects of the language used in the extract.

2) The sample question asks you specifically about the language used to show the tribe's suffering — so you shouldn't write about the language used to describe anything else.

3) You need to include technical terms when you're describing the writer's techniques.

4) Every point you make should be backed up with an example that's fully explained and developed — you could use P.E.E.D. to help you with this (see p.4).

5) Here are some things you could write about:

   • The effect of words and phrases, such as how specific verbs and adjectives are used (see p.34-35).

   • Language features and techniques, such as metaphors, similes and personification (see p.38-41).

   • The effect of different sentence forms, such as long or short sentences (see p.54-55).

Here's a **Grade 4-5** answer extract

It's great to include quotes, but try to keep them short.

> In the text it mentions that "**Their cracked lips and tongues were hard and leathery. Hunger gnawed their insides. They couldn't have spoken**". The fact that their lips and tongues are dry suggests that they don't have enough water, which makes you think they must be suffering.
>
> The extract also uses a **metaphor** and a simile which says that their thirst and tiredness "hung over them like a lead weight". **This makes their suffering sound like a burden, as lead weights are very heavy.**
>
> **The tribe is described as being "born of the desert", suggesting they have a special relationship with it. This is emphasised by the fact that "they could follow no other path".**

It's important to mention techniques like this, but you must always give an example and explain its effect.

This analyses the effect of the simile and relates it to the tribe's suffering.

This last paragraph isn't relevant to the question — it needs to be clearly linked back to the tribe's suffering.

1) This answer makes some good points about how the writer uses language to show the tribe's suffering and begins to use some technical terms.

2) It could be improved by explaining the effect of the language more fully, as it's not always clear how the examples are relevant to the question.

3) It could also do with looking at the effects of specific words or phrases more closely.

Graded Answers — Section A, Question 2

Here's a **Grade 6-7** answer extract

Referring to the writer shows that you understand they chose to use this language for a reason.

The writer says that the tribe's "cracked lips and tongues were hard and leathery". The fact that their lips are **"cracked"** demonstrates their thirst, but it also sounds painful, so it shows how much they are suffering. The writer also says that this thirst "hung over them like a lead weight". This simile suggests that thirst is a constant burden that the tribe cannot forget.

It's great to use short, embedded quotes like this.

It's really good to focus on the effects of specific words.

Imagery such as "Hunger gnawed their insides" highlights that the tribe's suffering is severe. **The verb "gnawed" personifies the hunger, which makes it seem like it is deliberately trying to hurt the tribe.** As a result, the tribe appears vulnerable, **which makes their suffering seem inescapable.**

It's important to keep linking the answer back to the question.

Repetition also reflects the tribe's suffering. The repetition of "nothing" and "no one" in the first sentence helps the reader to understand that **the tribe's suffering is partly emotional**, caused by the isolation and emptiness of the surrounding desert.

1) This answer makes some good points about the <u>effects</u> of the language the writer has chosen, which are <u>backed up</u> with appropriate quotations and <u>linked back</u> to the question.

2) It could be improved by analysing the <u>language features</u> and <u>techniques</u> in even more <u>detail</u>.

3) The final paragraph could also be <u>more clear</u> — it doesn't <u>analyse how</u> the repetition shows the tribe's emotional suffering.

This is a **Grade 8-9** answer extract

The answer uses a technical term correctly, and links its effect back to the question.

The tribe is **objectified** in the sentence that begins "The wind swept over them, through them", demonstrating that its people are at the mercy of the elements. **This makes their suffering seem inevitable and makes the tribe appear vulnerable.** This is emphasised by the personification of hunger, which "gnawed their insides". **The verb "gnawed" is reminiscent of a predator consuming its prey, which helps the reader to visualise the pain and hardship that the tribe are facing and perceive them as helpless victims.**

It's important to focus on the effect of the language.

This answer uses a good range of short quotes to back up the points.

The writer also uses short, simple sentences to mirror the tribe's exhaustion, for example **"They couldn't have spoken."** and **"They said nothing. Wanted nothing."** The length of these sentences makes the text abrupt, and reminds the reader of the slow, heavy footsteps of the tribe, highlighting their exhaustion. The repetition of "they" in these sentences is also used throughout the rest of the paragraph; this keeps the reader's attention focused on the **suffering of the tribe**, suggesting its presence is constant.

This answer stays focused on the question throughout.

1) This is a <u>really good</u> answer. It makes a range of perceptive points about the writer's <u>choice</u> of language and the <u>effect</u> it has, and then <u>develops</u> each point fully.

2) It also uses complex <u>technical terms</u> correctly and supports each point with relevant <u>quotations</u>.

Graded Answers — Section A, Question 3

The third question is also focused on language, but it's worth 5 more marks than the second question.

The **Third Question** looks like this

0	3	**Read lines 18-26.**

What impressions do you get of the men from these lines?

You must refer to the text to support your answer. **[10 marks]**

Think about how **Language** makes the reader **Feel**

1) The third question in section A is also about <u>language</u> and the <u>effects</u> it creates, but you're being asked to consider how language <u>influences the reader</u> as well.

2) This means you need to think about how the writer uses certain <u>words</u> or <u>techniques</u> to affect how the reader <u>feels</u> about the <u>men</u>.

Remember to always read the question carefully — it might only give you a specific part of the text to discuss.

3) Just like the second question, you could use <u>P.E.E.D.</u> to write your answer, and you need to use <u>technical terms</u> accurately.

4) You could <u>mention</u> some of these things:

- The effects of <u>specific words and phrases</u>, such as how particular verbs are used (see p.34-35).
- The effects of different <u>language features</u> such as similes and alliteration (see p.38-41).
- The effects of different <u>sentence forms</u>, such as long or short sentences (see p.54-55).
- How these techniques influence the reader's <u>attitude</u> and <u>emotions</u>.

Here's a **Grade 4-5** answer extract

In the passage, the writer uses alliteration when describing the men: "the blue clothing was in tatters, torn by thorns". **The words "tatters" and "torn" stand out, showing the difficulties the men have faced during their journey.** These words might also suggest that the men are poor.

The men seem **experienced and skilled**, as they "chose where their feet would come down without looking". This also makes it sound like they're sleepwalking, **which might suggest that they're feeling very tired.**

The writer describes the way the man holds the gun with "the barrel pointing upward like a flagpole", **which makes the reader think that he might be the leader of the men.** The text describes the other men as "brothers", which shows that they are close, so the reader feels curious about their relationship.

This is good — the effects of specific words are explained.

The paragraph begins with a clear point, which links back to the question.

This point could be improved by explaining more clearly how the language influences the reader's attitude.

This begins to analyse the impact of language on the reader, but it needs a clearer explanation.

1) This answer identifies some <u>language features</u> and describes some of their <u>effects</u>.

2) It could be improved by following the <u>P.E.E.D. structure</u> more closely — it needs to <u>explain</u> the effects in detail and <u>link</u> each point to the way the <u>men</u> are presented in the passage.

3) It also doesn't go into enough <u>detail</u> about how these features <u>influence</u> the reader.

Graded Answers — Section A, Question 3

Here's a **Grade 6-7** answer extract

The men appear unified in this passage. Despite the "weight of their burdens" they walk together, with one man holding a gun "like a flagpole". **This simile implies that the men are united in a purpose,** putting **the reader in the mind of a march to war and creating a sense of intrigue, as the reader is left wondering what it is that they are marching towards.**

This is a strong paragraph — it considers language, its effect and the impact this has on the reader.

The men are presented as accustomed to travelling the difficult route across the desert. The fact that they can follow "invisible trails", even though they can't see them, shows that they know the route well; this suggests to the reader that they have travelled in this direction many times before, as well as emphasising their skill at navigating the terrain.

The writer also makes the men seem weary. He describes how they are "bending slightly forward", **which emphasises the physical hardships that they are enduring and suggests that they are being gradually beaten down by them. This shows that their journey has been long and difficult.**

This explains the idea of the men being 'weary', but it doesn't go into enough detail about the effect this has on the reader.

1) This answer makes several good points about the <u>men</u>, and every point is <u>backed up</u> with <u>clearly-explained evidence</u> from the text.

2) The <u>effect</u> of the <u>language</u> on the <u>reader</u> is considered in places, but it doesn't do it <u>consistently</u> or in enough <u>detail</u>.

This is a **Grade 8-9** answer extract

Accurate use of technical terms makes the writing sound sophisticated.

The men are presented as fatigued and dishevelled, with their clothing "in tatters, torn by thorns". **The alliterative 't' sounds** create a harsh tone that emphasises the difficult reality of their lives; this encourages the reader to feel sympathy towards them. **This feeling of sympathy is furthered by the men's evident vulnerability;** the writer's assertion that "Only one of them carried a gun" implies that the tribe needs to protect itself, but only has limited means of doing so.

This develops a point about the way the language influences the reader's attitude towards the men.

It's great to analyse specific words like this.

The writer also emphasises that the men's ability to cross the desert is deeply ingrained within them, as they "chose where their feet would come down without looking." **The use of the verb "chose"** to describe their actions emphasises the deliberateness with which they decide their path, and the fact that they are able to place their steps "without looking" suggests that they are familiar with the desert trails. **This gives the reader the impression** that, despite all the hardships they face, there is a certainty about their progress.

This clearly links the point back to the question.

This is a <u>really good</u> answer — it makes <u>interesting</u> points about language and the way it affects the reader's impressions of the men. The points are <u>fully developed</u> and <u>technical terms</u> are used accurately.

Graded Answers — Section A, Question 4

Now it's time for the fourth question — it asks you to analyse the effects of structure and language.

Have another look at the **Fourth Question**

| 0 | 4 | **Read lines 27-39.** |

How does the writer make these lines mysterious?

You should write about:

- the writer's use of language to create mystery;
- how the text's structure builds mystery;
- the effects on the reader. **[10 marks]**

Link your points back to the **Effect** on the **Reader**

1) The fourth question in section A asks about how the writer uses <u>language</u> and <u>structure</u> to make lines 27-39 of the text <u>mysterious</u>.

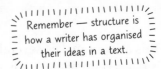
Remember — structure is how a writer has organised their ideas in a text.

2) When answering this question, you need to include <u>technical terms</u>, and you should use <u>P.E.E.D</u>.

3) To get top marks, you need to write about <u>everything</u> the bullet points mention:

- How <u>language features</u> and <u>specific words</u> (see p.34-35 and p.38-40) create a sense of <u>mystery</u>.
- How the <u>structure</u> (see p.52-53) of the text makes it seem more <u>mysterious</u>.
- You also need to write about how these techniques influence the reader's <u>attitude</u> and <u>emotions</u>.

Here's a **Grade 4-5** answer extract

The paragraph begins by linking the point back to the question.

The writer creates a sense of mystery because it isn't clear why the tribe are travelling. The valley they are heading towards is described as "waterless, shadeless", but the tribe seem to be heading in that direction. **This makes the tribe seem mysterious and confusing, as the reader doesn't understand why they have decided to make such an apparently illogical decision.**

Repetition is used to describe the tribe as "of the sand, of the wind, of the light, of the night". This makes it seem like the tribe are a part of nature.

The image of the men and women appearing "as if in a dream at the top of a dune" uses alliteration, which makes the words stand out from the rest of the text. This emphasises that the tribe seem dream-like — it's as if they are not real, which makes the text even more mysterious.

It's important to mention the effect on the reader, but this could go into a bit more detail about how the language creates this effect.

This paragraph mentions the effect of a structural feature, but it doesn't clearly explain how it makes this part of the text mysterious.

1) This answer discusses both <u>structure</u> and <u>language</u>, and starts to consider their <u>effects</u>.

2) However, it doesn't go into enough <u>detail</u> — it needs to explain more clearly how the <u>writer's techniques</u> create these effects.

3) It also needs to focus more on the <u>topic</u> in the question — not all the points are clearly linked to why the text feels <u>mysterious</u>.

Graded Answers — Section A, Question 4

This is a **Grade 6-7** answer extract

There is a contrast between the fifth and sixth paragraphs of the text. The fifth paragraph uses figurative language to describe the tribe and their journey, comparing the desert to the "waves" of the sea and referring to the "glow of the Milky Way". In the sixth paragraph, however, the focus is on more everyday topics, such as the "grayish-brown goats and sheep". This focus on small, mundane elements of the tribespeople's lives helps to **emphasise the mystery of the previous paragraph** by providing a contrast for the reader.

This sense of mystery in the extract is emphasised by the writer's description of the desert. Its **"inaccessible horizon"** makes it sound vast and complex. This is combined with the mention of "ancient tracks", which hints at the desert's long history. The writer uses these phrases to emphasise how little the reader knows about the desert, **which increases the sense of mystery that surrounds it.**

This makes a clear point about structure and links its effects back to the question.

Good use of a brief quote to back up a point.

The points in this answer are clearly linked back to the question.

1) This answer explores how a sense of <u>mystery</u> is created in the passage, looking at the effects of both <u>language</u> and <u>structure</u>. Each paragraph <u>links</u> back to the question.

2) It could be improved by <u>analysing</u> the writer's techniques in even more <u>detail</u>.

Here's a **Grade 8-9** answer extract

The writer creates a sense of mystery through the use of imagery, linking the tribe to huge concepts such as nature, heaven and space. The tribe were born directly **"of the cloudless sky"**, linking them to gods and the heavens; they were the people **"of the sand, of the wind, of the light"**, which links the tribe to all of nature; finally, they carried with them **"the glow of the Milky Way, the moon"**, which broadens their link to the greater universe and makes them seem almost ethereal. These images create a **dramatic sense of mystery** by making the tribe seem so much more than mere people, which in turn **makes the reader question their presence.**

This feeling of unreality is emphasised by the writer's complex use of sentence construction in the long sentence on lines 29-32. This introduces a series of images in quick succession, which mimics the uneven pace and illogical sequence of dreams, and creates a complex **mosaic** of images for the reader. This adds to the sense of mystery in the passage by making the text feel less rooted in real life, as the reader experiences the dreamlike sequencing of the description.

This answer looks at the specific effects of lots of parts of the language, and links them all back to the question.

The effect on the reader is covered for each point.

More complex vocabulary makes this answer stand out.

1) This answer makes perceptive points about both <u>structure</u> and <u>language</u>, and their <u>effects</u>.

2) It goes into lots of <u>detail</u> and uses technical terms <u>accurately</u>.

Graded Answers — Section A, Question 5

The fifth question in section A is worth another 10 marks, and is the last question in the section.

Remind yourself of the **Fifth Question**

> **0 5** **Read lines 40 to the end.**
>
> "In the last two paragraphs of this passage, the writer encourages the reader to feel sympathy for the tribe."
>
> To what extent do you agree with this view?
>
> You should write about:
> - your own impressions of the tribe and its surroundings, both here and in the passage as a whole;
> - how the writer has created these impressions.
>
> *You must refer to the text to support your answer.*   **[10 marks]**

Write about whether you **Agree** with the statement and **Why**

1) This question asks you to <u>evaluate</u> the text by saying how much you <u>agree</u> with the statement. This means you need to explain <u>how much</u> the lines make the reader feel <u>sympathy</u> for the tribe, and <u>how</u> the writer achieves this.

2) You need to <u>back up</u> your opinion using evidence from the text.

3) The bullet points under the question tell you what you <u>should</u> include in your answer:

> - You need to write about <u>your own feelings</u> — particularly about the tribe.
> - You also need to write about the <u>techniques</u> the writer uses to create these feelings, i.e. the <u>language</u> or <u>structural devices</u> they use.

You should focus on the lines the question specifies, but mention other parts of the passage to support your answer.

Here's a **Grade 4-5** answer extract

I think that the statement is true: the reader is encouraged to feel sympathy for the tribe. The narrator isn't clear about how long the tribe have been travelling: "months, years maybe". This makes it seem like they have been travelling for too long to remember accurately, and have had a hard life, so I feel sorry for them.

This is good — it gives an opinion on the statement.

The reader feels sorry for the tribe because their life is clearly very tough, partly because of the heat. The writer talks about how the sunlight "blazed" on line 49, and elsewhere in the passage it is also described as "burning". The reader gets the sense that the tribe's environment is unfriendly and dangerous.

Mentioning other parts of the passage shows that you're thinking about the text as a whole.

This hasn't explained how the words 'blazed' and 'burning' make the tribe's environment seem dangerous.

The image of the animals with their "throats slit open" and "left to rot" makes the reader feel sympathetic because it is disgusting. The fact that this has happened increases the reader's sympathy for the trials the tribe have gone through.

This mentions the effect on the reader, but doesn't clearly explain how the text creates this effect.

1) This answer starts to <u>comment</u> on the tribe's issues, and how this makes the <u>reader</u> feel sympathy for them.

2) This answer should be <u>developed</u> further by explaining <u>how</u> the language and structure <u>affect</u> the reader.

Graded Answers — Section A, Question 5

Here's a **Grade 6-7** answer extract

I strongly agree that the writer of the text creates sympathy for the travellers. It is made clear that the tribe have no choice but to continue on their difficult journey when the writer explains that the tribe "must walk even farther". The word "must" emphasises that this is a necessity rather than a choice; this makes the reader feel sympathy for the tribe because they seem forced to endure difficult conditions, with no way to avoid them.

The difficulty of their lives is emphasised by the use of a long sentence on lines 40-44, in which the narrator lists a series of routes they've followed. The length of this sentence mirrors the length of the tribe's journey, and the list of places, tribes and regions creates a relentless tone that suggests the tribe haven't been able to properly rest or stop for a long time. This increases the reader's sympathy by emphasising the prolonged difficulties that the tribe have had to face.

This shows that you've thought about the extent to which you agree with the statement.

This answer picks out specific words and comments on their impact.

This clearly explains the effect that the language creates.

1) This answer clearly focuses on <u>how</u> the writer creates <u>sympathy</u> for the tribe.

2) It uses a good range of relevant <u>quotes</u> as evidence, and <u>develops</u> the points by relating them to the effect on the <u>reader</u>.

This is a **Grade 8-9** answer extract

The writer is highly successful in creating sympathy for the tribe. This is achieved by emphasising the harsh environment of the desert. For example, he uses a metaphor, describing the available water as a "sweat mark on the surface of the desert", which had to be "wrenched from the sand". By comparing water to "sweat", the writer links finding water to hard work; this impression is reinforced by the verb "wrenched", which implies hard effort and powerful movements. By focusing on something that many people take for granted, and illustrating how difficult it is for the tribespeople to acquire it, the writer clearly emphasises the difficulties of desert life; this may invoke the reader's sympathy because it contrasts with their own life experiences.

The harsh desert environment is also emphasised by the reference to "the meager gift of an arid God" on lines 55-56. The adjective "meager" makes the reader feel sympathy for the tribe, as it suggests that they are forced to survive on limited resources. The subsequent reference to the water as the "gift" of a god is used ironically, as that gift will cause illnesses such as "colic, vomiting". This makes the reader feel even more sympathy for the tribe, because it suggests that even their god cannot or will not help them.

This answer gives a clear response to the statement, then goes on to explain how the writer achieves this effect.

This shows an understanding of how the text's language affects the reader's response.

This analyses the language used in the extract in detail.

Keep referring back to the statement to make sure your answer is focused.

This is a <u>top grade</u> answer — it clearly responds to the <u>statement</u> in an <u>original</u> way, and its points are backed up with relevant <u>quotes</u> and <u>examples</u>.

Graded Answers — Section B

There's a choice of four tasks in section B — go for one that inspires you, but don't waste lots of time deciding.

The **Section B** question looks like this

| 1 | 1 |

*In this section, you will be assessed for the quality of your **creative prose writing** skills.*

Choose **one** of the following titles for your writing:
Either, *(a)* Taking a Chance
Or, *(b)* The Cabin
Or, *(c)* Write about a time when you were at a theme park.
Or, *(d)* Write a story which ends:
"…We never discussed the mysterious events of that night again." **[40 marks]**

Your writing needs to **Interest** the **Reader**

1) The purpose of creative writing is always to entertain the reader. You need to use a range of sophisticated vocabulary and language techniques that will be interesting for the reader.

2) Your writing should have an interesting plot and characters, and be really descriptive — make sure you describe the scene and the characters in an engaging and detailed way.

> For top marks, your plot and characters need to be original and well-developed.

3) The structure of your writing is really important. You need to write in a way that is intriguing to the reader and keeps them gripped throughout your story.

4) There are loads of marks on offer for spelling, punctuation and grammar in this question, so it's really important to write accurately (see pages 9-10).

Here's a **Grade 4-5** answer extract

The small house stood on its own, surrounded by fir trees and rocks. Snow had gathered against the walls in deep piles. It did not look very inviting, but to Anneka it was the most welcome sight in the world. She had got lost in the woods and she had been worried that she would have to spend the night outside in the forest, which was freezing cold and **as scary as a spider's nest.**

Anneka walked towards the door and knocked. To her surprise the door swung open and she could see inside the house. She saw a single room with a fire burning in the fireplace and a table set for two, with hot food piled high on the plates. There was only one thing missing from the scene, there were no people inside.

Anneka walked **tentatively** into the room and began to warm her hands in front of the fire, wondering where the people who lived in the house had gone. The room looked as if someone had just stepped out, but the only path Anneka had seen was the one she had come along, and she had not passed anyone else. **Surely they couldn't have just disappeared?**

This sets the scene, but it could do with some more imaginative description.

It's good to use descriptive techniques like similes, but this one isn't very original and it doesn't really create the right tone.

The punctuation in this sentence isn't quite right — a colon would fit better.

This is a good piece of descriptive vocabulary.

This sets up a mystery, which makes the reader want to know what has happened.

1) This answer has a fairly clear structure and gets straight into the story.

2) However, it lacks description, and the vocabulary isn't very varied. The character in the story could also be developed further to give the reader a better sense of her personality or appearance.

Graded Answers — Section B

Here's a **Grade 6-7** answer extract

This uses the opening sentence of the story to set the scene nicely.

> Robin lowered the axe he had been using to chop wood and peered towards the mountains, his eyes squinting in the sharp orange glow of the slowly setting sun. He was sure he had seen a movement up there, **a flash of scarlet against the sparkling white of the snow-capped peaks.** But who would be mad enough to venture into the mountains at dusk, in winter, with snow and freezing temperatures forecast that night?
>
> Robin sighed wearily, deciding that it must have been his imagination playing tricks on him, as it so often did out here in the mountains.
>
> A low, **ominous rumble echoed down the valley,** interrupting his thoughts. Robin froze momentarily, listening intently, **then snapped into action,** frantically gathering his tools as the sound grew louder and closer.
>
> The avalanche roared destructively and unstoppably towards his isolated home.

This answer uses interesting language to make the descriptions more vivid and to entertain the reader.

This uses the senses to help the reader to imagine the scene.

The change of pace creates excitement in this story.

1) This has a clear <u>structure</u>, uses good <u>descriptions</u> and builds <u>interest</u> for the reader.

2) It could be improved by using more <u>complex</u> sentence structures and a <u>wider range</u> of punctuation.

This is a **Grade 8-9** answer extract

> I surfaced suddenly from a dreamless sleep, the skin on my forearms tingling with an instinctive awareness that something was wrong. There — that noise again! A skittering, scrabbling, scuffling noise in the far corner of the dimly lit room. **I sat up in bed, the quilt clutched to my chest** with stone-numb hands, my breath forming foggy billows in the chilly air.
>
> **The sun was just rising; its feeble light trickled through the window, fractured into myriad rainbows by the intricate whorls and fingers of ice on the frosty pane.** As a brighter beam pierced the gloom, I gasped. There, huddled by the door, a young wolf cub gazed at me with sorrowful, strangely human eyes. His tawny fur was matted with blood, **as rich and red as the morning light that now illuminated it fully.**
>
> I eased myself out of the wooden bunk, crouched down on the splintered floorboards and held out a trembling hand towards the cub. He gazed at me uncertainly, then slowly, slowly, he stretched forward and snuffled at my fingers, his breath **as warm and ticklish as a damp feather duster.**

This beginning immediately sets the tone and atmosphere by creating tension.

This uses a first-person narrator to establish a strong connection with the reader.

Vivid description and interesting vocabulary help to set the scene.

Unusual imagery helps to set this answer apart.

1) This has a structure that <u>interests</u> the reader by <u>slowly revealing</u> what's going on.

2) It's also packed with imaginative <u>imagery</u> and unusual <u>vocabulary</u> to make it more <u>entertaining</u> to read, which helps it to fit the <u>purpose</u> of the question.

Sample Exam — Paper 2

These two pages show you some example questions that are like the ones you'll see in paper 2 — the texts to go with the questions in section A are on pages 100-101. First have a read through the questions and the texts, then have a look at the handy graded answer extracts we've provided on pages 102-115.

Section A — Reading

Section A: 40 marks

These questions are only worth one mark each, so you just need to write the answers (in quotes or your own words) and nothing else.

Read the 21st-century newspaper article by Rishi Sunak on page 100.

1 1
(a) How many teachers and governors attended the education forum? **[1 mark]**

(b) When this article was written, how long ago had the education funding formula been dropped? **[1 mark]**

(c) In 2014, how much less funding did a pupil in North Yorkshire receive compared to a pupil in Middlesbrough? **[1 mark]**

You're asked to find specific bits of information, so you need to read the questions and the text carefully.

'How' questions are about the methods the writer uses and their effect on the reader.

1 2
How does Rishi Sunak try to convince us that education funding needs to be more fairly distributed?

You should comment on:
- what he says to **influence readers**;
- his use of **language, tone and structure.** **[10 marks]**

This question asks you about the effect that the text has on the reader.

You need to write about language, tone and structure for this question.

To answer the following questions, you will need to read the extract from the 19th-century article by Lawton B. Evans on page 101.

These questions ask you to show that you can find and understand implicit and explicit information from the text.

1 3
(a) What does the writer mean by "volcanic genius breaks through the hard crust" in line 12? **[1 mark]**

(b) What does the writer suggest has caused the lack of development in rural areas? **[2 marks]**

Part (b) is worth two marks, so there should be two reasons in the answer.

1 4
What do you think and feel about Lawton B. Evans's views on cities and the country?

You should comment on:
- what is said;
- **how it is said.**
You must refer to the text to support your comments. **[10 marks]**

You need to comment on the techniques the writer uses to convey his ideas.

This question asks you to evaluate the text by giving your opinion on the writer's views.

It's important to include plenty of evidence from the text for this question.

Sample Exam — Paper 2

To answer the following questions you will need to use both texts.

You need to write a summary — a piece of writing that combines ideas from both texts, but is written using your own words.

| 1 | 5 |
According to these two writers, why does education in rural areas need to be focused on? **[4 marks]**

| 1 | 6 |
Both of these texts are about education. **Compare the following:**

- the writers' attitudes to education;

- **how they get across their arguments.**

You must use the text to support your comments and make it clear which text you are referring to.

This question asks you to compare, so you need to write about how the writers' viewpoints are similar or different.

You need to write about how the writers use language and structure to achieve effects. **[10 marks]**

Section B — Writing

This section requires you to answer both writing questions.

Section B: 40 marks

In this section, you will be assessed for the quality of your writing skills.

For each question, 12 marks are awarded for communication and organisation; 8 marks are awarded for vocabulary, sentence structure, punctuation and spelling.

You should aim to write about 300-400 words for each task.

For writing questions, you get marks for how you write (i.e. language and structure) and the accuracy of your writing (i.e. your spelling, punctuation and grammar).

| 2 | 1 |
Your school wants to encourage students to take up more outdoor hobbies.

Write a report for the school governors suggesting ways this might be done.

You could include:

- **examples of hobbies that students might enjoy;**

- **ideas for persuading students to take them up.**

This question tells you the form (a report) and the audience (the school governors). **[20 marks]**

Your answer needs to incorporate both of these bullet points.

| 2 | 2 |
Your local council wants to encourage young people to have part-time jobs before the age of sixteen.

You are going to write an article for a broadsheet newspaper to share your views on this idea. You could agree or disagree with the council's idea.

Write an engaging article for a **broadsheet newspaper giving your views.** **[20 marks]**

You need to write a newspaper article for this question, but it asks you to give your opinion — so it needs to be written like a commentary rather than a news report (see p.73).

You don't have to actually answer these questions...

On the next two pages, you'll find the two source texts — make sure you read them carefully. Then use the sample answers on pages 102-115 to build your understanding of how to write great paper 2 answers.

21st-Century Source

Here are the exam sources to go with the questions on pages 98-99. On this page is a newspaper article written by an MP (Member of Parliament) called Rishi Sunak, which was published in October 2015.

Rishi Sunak: Why rural schools must receive a fairer deal on funding

ONE of my constituents summed it up best. Their belief was that education is the greatest single tool to allow you to change your own life and make an impact in your community.

5 My grandparents grew up on the other side of the world with very little. Two generations later, I have the incredible privilege of being a Member of Parliament. Many of us can tell similar stories of where our families started, what they worked to achieve and how their
10 efforts passed something on to the next generation. I am confident that all these journeys are built on the foundation of a strong education.

However, since becoming a Member of Parliament, it has become clear to me that our current means of distributing funding between schools is, at best, out of date and, at worst, unfair for our rural schools and local children.

15 This week I hosted an education forum with more than 50 local primary school teachers and governors to learn about their experiences. We agreed to work together and launch a campaign to fight for a better deal.

Many of our children and grandchildren attend wonderful village primary schools that are the beating hearts of their communities. But because of the nature of our countryside and the distances between
20 settlements, these schools will often be small.

There are particular costs of providing education in small rural settings that are often not well understood by policy-makers sitting in Whitehall. For example, it is often difficult to organise seven primary school year groups into a standard class structure and sometimes an additional half class is needed. More obviously, small schools cannot spread the cost of administration or leadership over a
25 large number of pupils.

The way funding was allocated between schools historically did not adequately recognise these factors. This led to significant problems in under-funded areas, in particular the East Riding* a decade ago, where there was talk of four-day weeks and mass redundancies.

Although people often talk about problems with the education funding formula, the reality is that
30 there is no formula. In response to crises like the one in East Riding, it was dropped a decade ago and, instead, whatever a local authority received then has been either uniformly increased or decreased.

So if your local area was under-funded 10 years ago, it will continue to be. If your local schools got a raw deal back then, they most likely still will do now. What was a temporary fix is now long overdue for reform.

35 Today two children, both on free school meals but living in different places, can receive very different sums of money for their education. Schools around the country that are similar can get very different budgets and children with the same needs can receive very different levels of financial support.

Last year, a pupil in my constituency in North Yorkshire received £500 less than a pupil only a few miles away in Middlesbrough. In the case of a city such as Manchester, the gap is as high as £700. A
40 pupil in one of the top five funded areas received over £2,000 more than North Yorkshire does.

This simply needs to change. In a climate where money is tight as we balance the books, it is even more important that schools receive their fair share.

At the forum I heard inspiring stories of what heads, teachers and governors are doing to ensure our local schools can continue to thrive. They all deserve their fair share of funding so they can continue to
45 do the vital job they do so well.

Providing a fairly funded and excellent education is one of this generation's most important responsibilities to undertake for the benefit of the next generation. We simply must get it right.

Glossary
* East Riding — a part of the county of Yorkshire in the north of England

19th-Century Source

This is the second exam source, which is an extract from an article published in a journal in 1896. It was written by Lawton B. Evans, an American teacher and educational leader.

THE COUNTY UNIT IN EDUCATIONAL ORGANIZATION

By Lawton B. Evans, Superintendent of Schools, Augusta, Ga.

The educational thought of our time has been chiefly directed toward the improvement of city school systems. So we hear of the great schools at Boston, Chicago, New York, Cincinnati, Philadelphia, and a score of other places; but I have yet to hear of a single county or township of rural population, the excellence of whose schools entitles them to national repute. The emphasis of our thought has been
5 placed long and devotedly on city schools at the expense of the rural schools.

It is true that cities are the centers of highest civilization. Our human nature has made them so. Architecture, art, literature, schools, fashion, reach their highest forms when people strive with each other for display. The very contact of people civilizes them. Cities are likewise the centers of greatest iniquity*. The worthless, the idle, the contentious, the wicked, gravitate toward large centers. Extremes of virtue
10 and vice meet. The force of cities attracts everything, good and bad alike. But cities do not develop individuality. There is a leveling influence about them that merges individuals into masses, and it is only occasionally that a volcanic genius breaks through the hard crust and thrusts itself above the burning level of great city life. The highest types of individuality, the strong and independent men of our nation, have been born and bred in village or rural homes, away from the turmoil of city life, in quiet and serious
15 communion with nature, in her grand and ennobling forms. It is out of the rural homes that the great men of our country have come. Genius abhors the palace and the crowded cities and the cradles of luxury, and courts the cabins and the open fields and the simple but stern homes of the poor.

We need skilled labor in the fields as well as in the city. We need intelligent and scientific management of a farm as well as of a great factory. We need business methods here as well as in
20 the great commercial houses of the city. We need economy of effort and conservation of force and adaptation of invention and discovery here, if we need it anywhere. And we need culture and refinement among the country people. Music, painting, books, and all the evidences of a higher kind of life are as proper on the farms as in the cities. The more highly educated the people of the rural districts are, the more capable they will be of taking advantage of the improvement in machinery, of economizing time and
25 labor in producing raw material, and the more time they will have to devote to culture and the higher arts of civilization. They will accomplish as much as now in far less time, and will live more comfortably and more happily.

That farm life is behind city life in development is due in some part to the isolation of the rural population. Men live too far apart and see each other too seldom to exert a refining influence over each
30 other. In other part, it is due to the attention that has been given to educating the people of the city.

It is quite time that we change the emphasis of our study, turn aside from the contemplation of the excellences of the city schools, and consider the necessities of the rural schools. The wisest policy is to frame some educational scheme that will keep the people in the country, that will stop the exodus from the farms, that will make the rural population content, that will make them enlightened and prosperous.

Glossary
* iniquity — sin

Graded Answers — Section A, Question 1

The first question is pretty straightforward — it asks you to find information from the text for three marks.

Here's a reminder of the First Question

1 1	(a)	How many teachers and governors attended the education forum?	**[1 mark]**
	(b)	When this article was written, how long ago had the education funding formula been dropped?	**[1 mark]**
	(c)	In 2014, how much less funding did a pupil in North Yorkshire receive compared to a pupil in Middlesbrough?	**[1 mark]**

The question is in Three Parts

1) The first question in section A asks you to answer <u>three</u> short questions about the <u>first text</u> — the newspaper article by Rishi Sunak.

2) This question is testing the ability to <u>find information and ideas</u> in the text

3) There's <u>one</u> mark available for each part of the question, so you just need to write down <u>one fact</u>. There's no need to <u>analyse</u> the facts or give any <u>extra information</u>.

4) The questions ask you to find facts from <u>any part</u> of the text, so you need to read the whole text <u>thoroughly</u> to find the right information.

Here's a Grade 4-5 answer

Part (a) has been answered <u>correctly</u> here, but (b) and (c) are <u>wrong</u>, so this answer would only get <u>one</u> mark.

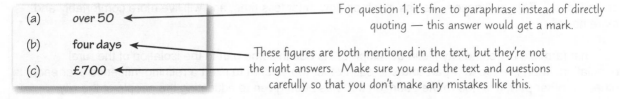

(a)	over 50	←	For question 1, it's fine to paraphrase instead of directly quoting — this answer would get a mark.
(b)	four days	←	These figures are both mentioned in the text, but they're not the right answers. Make sure you read the text and questions carefully so that you don't make any mistakes like this.
(c)	£700	←	

This is a Grade 6-7 answer

Parts (a) and (b) have been answered <u>correctly</u> here, but part (c) is <u>wrong</u>. This answer would get <u>two</u> marks.

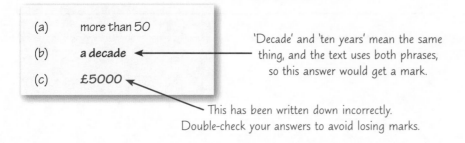

(a)	more than 50	
(b)	a decade	← 'Decade' and 'ten years' mean the same thing, and the text uses both phrases, so this answer would get a mark.
(c)	£5000	←

This has been written down incorrectly. Double-check your answers to avoid losing marks.

Graded Answers — Section A, Question 2

It's time for the second question — the next two pages show you how you could answer it.

The **Second Question** looks like this

1	2

How does Rishi Sunak try to convince us that education funding needs to be more fairly distributed?

You should comment on:
- what he says to influence readers;
- his use of language, tone and structure.

[10 marks]

This question is about how the **Writer Influences** the **Reader**

1) The second question in section A asks you about <u>how</u> the writer achieves their <u>purpose</u> — to <u>persuade</u> the reader to agree with their point of view.

2) This means you need to comment on the writer's <u>techniques</u>, and explain the <u>effect</u> that they have on the reader.

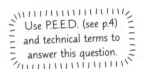
Use P.E.E.D. (see p.4) and technical terms to answer this question.

3) To do this, you need to write about <u>each</u> of the things mentioned in the <u>bullet points</u>. For this question, you would have to:

- Write about the <u>points</u> Rishi Sunak makes to <u>persuade</u> the reader to agree with him.
- Explain how <u>language techniques</u> (see p.33-35 and p.38-44) are used to <u>persuade</u> the reader.
- Write about how the <u>tone</u> (see p.32) and <u>structure</u> (see p.51) of the text <u>persuade</u> the reader.

4) You also need to include <u>quotes</u> and <u>examples</u> from the text to back up each point that you make.

This is a **Grade 4-5** answer extract

The reader wants to agree with Rishi Sunak because he says he is a "Member of Parliament", which suggests that he is an expert in understanding political matters. **This makes the reader more easily persuaded by anything that he says because they think they should trust his opinion.**

    The writer also uses words like "obviously" and "simply" to make it seem like everybody should agree with him. This makes the reader trust the writer even more and agree **that the government needs to change the way that schools receive money, especially in rural areas like North Yorkshire that get a "raw deal".**

    The article has a conclusion that sums up the argument: the writer says that "fairly funded and excellent" education is an "important" responsibility, **so the reader will clearly remember the writer's main argument.**

This comments on the effect that the text has on the reader.

The way this bit is written is too long-winded, and needs to be more focused on the question.

It needs to be more clearly explained how the conclusion helps to make the article more persuasive.

1) This answer makes some points about <u>how</u> the writer <u>convinces</u> the reader to agree with his point of view.

2) However, some of the examples need to be <u>explained</u> more clearly and in more detail.

3) This answer could also be improved by including more <u>technical terms</u>.

Graded Answers — Section A, Question 2

Here's a **Grade 6-7** answer extract

The writer of the newspaper article uses several real-life examples to illustrate his point that rural schools are currently underfunded. These give the text a trustworthy, factual tone that makes the reader more likely to agree with the writer's argument. This is reinforced by his inclusion of statistics: the idea that some pupils receive "over £2,000 more" than others demonstrates that the way schools are funded currently is unfair, which makes the reader think it needs to be changed. **The numbers also shock the reader, which might further persuade them to agree with Sunak's argument.**

The structure of the article also helps to convince the reader to agree with Sunak's argument. For example, the extract ends with a short, simple sentence: "We simply must get it right." This has a powerful impact on the reader, because it adds to the reader's impression that Sunak's argument is uncomplicated: it is "simply" the right thing to do to change the way that educational funding is distributed.

This is good — it starts with a clear point, then discusses the effect on the reader.

This point has been really well developed by linking together different examples and their effects.

For this question, it's important to comment on language and structure.

1) This answer clearly analyses the effect that the text has on the reader.
2) It could be improved by analysing the writer's use of language in more detail.

Here's a **Grade 8-9** answer extract

Rishi Sunak's article is structured so that it persuades the reader. It begins by using a short, emphatic first paragraph, which is used to immediately establish the key idea that education is the "greatest single tool" at our disposal. The superlative **"greatest"** shows the importance that Sunak places on education, and the fact that the idea is paraphrased from a "constituent" indicates that other people agree with Sunak's beliefs; **this makes the reader more likely to be convinced by his argument.**

After establishing the importance of education, Sunak then goes on to explain how a lack of funding is putting some children's education at risk. To illustrate this, he balances shocking statistics, such as the "£2,000" funding gap between children in different constituencies, with authoritative statements such as "This simply needs to change." These elements combine to create a **confident, assured tone** that helps to persuade the reader that Sunak's argument is justified.

Sunak also tries to persuade the reader using direct address, which is reinforced by the use of a repetitive sentence structure. The repetition of "If your local area" and "If your local schools" continually places emphasis on the word "your", which persuades the reader by suggesting that they could be individually affected by unfair funding.

This is great — the effects of specific vocabulary choices are analysed in detail.

It's important to link your answers back to the question.

It's great to comment on the tone of a text as part of your analysis.

This answer consistently refers back to the effect that the text has on the reader.

This answer makes a range of well-developed and perceptive points that clearly answer the question.

Graded Answers — Section A, Question 3

The third question in section A is another fairly short question — it's split into two parts and is worth three marks. The questions ask you to pick out a few key details from the 19th-century text.

Here's the **Third Question** again

1	3

    (a) What does the writer mean by "volcanic genius breaks through the hard crust" in line 12?   **[1 mark]**

    (b) What does the writer suggest has caused the lack of development in rural areas?   **[2 marks]**

You need to **Choose** information **Carefully**

1) The third question in section A asks you to answer <u>two</u> short questions about the journal article by Lawton B. Evans.

2) It's testing the ability to <u>find</u> and <u>understand</u> information and ideas in the text.

3) For part (a) you just need to <u>explain</u> what the phrase <u>means</u>, with no <u>extra analysis</u>.

4) Part (b) is worth <u>two marks</u>, so the answer should give <u>two</u> reasons. There's no need to <u>analyse</u> the reasons or give any <u>extra information</u>.

5) You need to read the questions carefully, as they might be about something that is <u>implicit</u> — information that isn't stated outright, but is <u>implied</u> by what the text says.

Here's a **Grade 4-5** answer

Part (a) has been answered <u>incorrectly</u> here, and there's only <u>one</u> correct answer given for part (b). This answer would get <u>one</u> mark.

(a)	It's a metaphor.	This answer doesn't explain what the phrase <u>means</u>, so it doesn't get a mark.
(b)	Rural populations are very isolated.	Part (b) is worth <u>two</u> marks, so you need to pick out two details from the text. This answer is only worth one mark.

And here's a **Grade 8-9** answer

This answer has the <u>correct responses</u> for parts (a) <u>and</u> (b) — it gets <u>full marks</u>.

It's fine to paraphrase or quote from the text, as long as the answer is accurate.

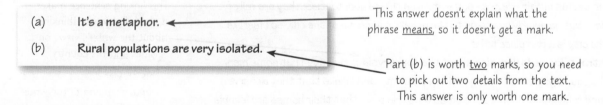

(a)	Someone special rises above the "leveling" influence of the cities.
(b)	People who live in rural areas are isolated from each other.
	Too much attention has been given to educating people in the cities.

You only need to give two reasons to get full marks, even if there are more in the text.

Graded Answers — Section A, Question 4

The fourth question is all about evaluating the text — have a look at these sample answers.

Here's a reminder of the **Fourth Question**

| 1 | 4 | What do you think and feel about Lawton B. Evans's views on cities and the country?
You should comment on:
  • what is said;
  • how it is said.
You must refer to the text to support your comments. [10 marks] |

Think about the writer's **Choice Of Words**

1) The fourth question in section A is about your <u>personal response</u> to the writer's viewpoint. You need to <u>evaluate</u> the text by explaining your <u>thoughts</u> and <u>feelings</u> about the topic in the question.

2) For every <u>point</u> you make about <u>what</u> the writer has said, you also need to explain <u>how</u> the writer has used <u>language</u> and <u>structure</u> to convey their views.

> Your evidence can either be paraphrased or quoted directly from the text — see page 5 for more about this.

3) The question reminds you to refer to the <u>text</u> in your answers, so you also need to use plenty of <u>evidence</u> from the text to back up each point.

4) To write a <u>really good</u> answer to this question, you need to show that you've <u>engaged</u> with the text — you need to express a detailed, clear <u>understanding</u> of the writer's viewpoint.

Here's a **Grade 4-5** answer extract

Here, it needs to be explained how the text has this effect on the reader.

   I think that Lawton B. Evans is too harsh on cities. He thinks that "genius" can't emerge as easily in a city, and that some of the people there are "worthless" and "idle". **This seems unfair.** He does say some nice things about cities: they are full of "civilization", but he quickly moves on to the negative aspects of the city so I feel like, overall, the city is a bad place to be.

This linking sentence makes it clear that you're thinking about the writer's views on cities <u>and</u> the country.

   In contrast, Evans is very nice about the countryside. He says that some men born in the countryside are "strong and independent", and thinks that they deserve "culture and refinement" just like the cities have. He says that their homes are "simple" and "stern" though, which makes the countryside seem like a bad place to live. Overall I think I prefer Evans's description of the countryside to the city, **because it seems a lot more relaxing than the "Extremes of virtue and vice" that you see in cities.**

This answer doesn't show a clear understanding of the writer's views and their purpose. The text wasn't about how relaxing cities and the countryside are — it was about why the countryside should receive more attention.

1) This starts to answer the <u>question</u> — it gives an <u>evaluation</u> of the text by commenting on how the reader thinks and feels about the writer's views.

2) Both the <u>city</u> and <u>countryside</u> are commented on, and relevant <u>examples</u> are used to support each point.

3) There's room for <u>improvement</u> though — it needs to be explained <u>how</u> the writer's techniques have particular effects on the reader. It would also be better to use more <u>effective</u> and <u>sophisticated</u> vocabulary, e.g. 'positive' instead of 'nice'.

Graded Answers — Section A, Question 4

Here's a **Grade 6-7** answer extract

Evans presents a view of cities that is a combination of praise and condemnation. His use of violent imagery, such as the image of the "genius" breaking through the "hard crust" makes the reader feel like life in the city is violent and repressive. In contrast though, he repeats the superlative adjective "highest" in reference to the cities; this repetition emphasises his belief that cities can be a place where culture and civilisation reach their pinnacle. These opposing descriptions of the city combine overall **to make cities seem hectic and stressful.**

In contrast to the cities, Evans presents the countryside as having a calming influence over its inhabitants. He describes the "quiet and serious communion" that can be had with nature; the combination of gentle adjectives in this phrase shows the peacefulness of nature. Evans presents this peace as very positive because it allows **"genius"** to flourish, which contrasts with the **"leveling"** influence of the cities.

This is good — it clearly evaluates the way that cities are presented in the text.

This describes the way that the text makes the reader feel, which links it back to the question.

Short, embedded quotes are used to support points without disturbing the flow of the answer.

1) This answer gives a <u>clear evaluation</u> of the text, backed up by <u>relevant examples</u>.

2) It could be improved by linking the second paragraph back to the effect on the <u>reader</u>.

This is a **Grade 8-9** answer extract

Lawton B. Evans presents a complex set of views on both cities and the country, which ultimately helps him **to elucidate the importance of rural areas.**

He makes it clear that there are impressive aspects of the city: for example, he describes cities as "centers of highest civilization"; this hyperbole indicates his admiration for the culture and art which flourishes in the city. However, he also describes the "leveling influence" of the city, which "merges individuals into masses". The alliterative 'm' sound in this phrase **emphasises the amalgamating qualities of the city to the reader, leaving them with the impression that cities are somewhat restrictive and confining.**

On the other hand, Evans portrays life in the countryside as "behind" in "development", which contrasts with the "civilization" of the cities. However, unlike the city, Evans believes that the countryside is set up to produce "The highest types of individuality". **The adjective "ennobling", used to describe the effect of the countryside, links rural life to the lives of nobles and the aristocracy, and emphasises how influential Evans thinks the countryside can be in developing "great" individuals.** These contrasts between the country and the city help Evans to persuade the reader that it is important to focus on rural areas, because they can have an important and influential effect on society.

Talking about the writer's purpose is a good way to introduce how the text affects the reader.

This describes clearly how the text makes the reader think and feel.

This analyses a key word in detail, which helps to support the point being made.

This answer makes some interesting and <u>original points</u>. It gives a good <u>overview</u> of the text as well as making detailed <u>points</u> about the effect it has on the reader.

Graded Answers — Section A, Question 5

The fifth question in section A is the first of two questions that ask you to write about both texts.

Here is the **Fifth Question** again

1	5	According to these two writers, why does education in rural areas need to be focused on? **[4 marks]**

Explain the **Writers' Viewpoints** on a particular topic

1) In your answer to the fifth question in section A, you need to show that you can <u>pick out information</u> from <u>both</u> sources about a particular topic, then summarise it in your <u>own words</u>.

2) Even though you're writing in your own words, you should still include <u>evidence</u> from the texts to support the points you're making.

3) The question asks you to pick out information about <u>education</u> in <u>rural areas</u> — so you should only include points that focus on that topic, and not anything else.

4) There's no need to <u>compare</u> the two writers' opinions — you just need to <u>explain</u> them clearly and fully, in as <u>concise</u> a way as possible.

5) This question is only worth <u>four marks</u>, so don't waste time giving lots of <u>unnecessary detail</u>.

> A summary is a piece of writing that combines the ideas from both texts — have a look at p.13 if you need a reminder.

Here's a **Grade 4-5** answer extract

Both writers think that rural education is important. Rishi Sunak thinks it needs to be focused on because lots of schools are currently "under-funded" and the problems are not "well understood". Lawton B. Evans, **on the other hand**, thinks that rural education needs improving because the countryside is underdeveloped: he says it is **"behind"** the city. **Evans also says that cities attract everything "good and bad alike".**

This does summarise something that both writers say, but to answer the question properly it needs to clearly summarise why both writers think this.

This isn't necessary — you don't need to make comparisons between the two texts for this question.

This is good — using short quotes as evidence from the text.

This point doesn't answer the question.

1) This makes some points about <u>both texts</u>, that are backed up by <u>relevant examples</u>.

2) It needs to stay <u>focused</u> on the question — some points <u>aren't relevant</u>.

3) It could also be improved by <u>combining</u> the writers' viewpoints so there's a clearer <u>overview</u> of the reasons why rural education needs to be focused on.

4) It should also avoid <u>comparing</u> the writers' viewpoints — this question just asks you to <u>summarise</u> what the writers are saying.

Graded Answers — Section A, Question 5

Here's a **Grade 6-7** answer extract

> Both writers suggest that rural schools need to be focused on because if they are improved it will have a positive impact on their whole communities. Rishi Sunak says that they are the "beating hearts" of small villages and that education is the most important thing to "make an impact". Lawton B. Evans says that improved rural education would make the rural population "content", "enlightened" and "prosperous".
>
> The writers also state that it's unfair that rural schools have been neglected in favour of the cities: Rishi Sunak **gives examples of the funding differences** between schools in different areas, and Lawton B. Evans says that development of urban schools has come **"at the expense"** of rural schools.

This makes a clear point that summarises something that both texts are saying.

You can paraphrase the text or quote it directly to support your points.

1) This clearly <u>summarises</u> some aspects of the writers' arguments, and some good <u>examples</u> are used from both texts to back up the points being made.

2) It could be improved by giving more of an <u>overview</u> of what both writers are saying.

Here's a **Grade 8-9** answer extract

This is a good opening — it shows that the answer is going to give an overview of the reasons given in both texts.

> The two writers give a variety of reasons to explain why education in rural areas needs to be more focused on. For example, they suggest that rural education needs to be focused on because the current situation is unfair. This is demonstrated by Sunak's description of the "raw deal" that many schools receive, and Evans's explanation that the development of city schools comes at the "expense" of rural schools.
>
> The writers also argue that rural education needs to be focused on because of the positive effect it could have on the wider community. Sunak says that education allows people to "make an impact" in their community, and Evans explains that improved rural education would increase productivity in the "fields" and on the "farm", thereby making them more "prosperous". In addition, Evans implies that focusing more on rural education would mean that society produced more "great men", because rural people would have more time to devote to "culture and the higher arts".
>
> It is therefore clear that rural education needs a greater focus because, if improved, it would have a positive impact on rural communities and society as a whole.

This sentence summarises the writers' viewpoints without comparing them.

This summarises the evidence in the paragraph in a concise way.

This is <u>great</u> — it gives a more comprehensive <u>overview</u> of the two writers' viewpoints, and it combines <u>both</u> writers' arguments in a <u>clear</u> and <u>concise</u> way.

Graded Answers — Section A, Question 6

The sixth question is worth another 10 marks and asks you to compare the texts.

Have another look at the **Sixth Question**

| 1 | 6 | Both of these texts are about education. Compare the following: |

* the writers' attitudes to education;
* how they get across their arguments.

You must use the text to support your comments and make it clear which text you are referring to.   **[10 marks]**

Compare the writers' different **Points of View**

1) The last question in section A is about what the writers <u>think</u> about education, and <u>how they show</u> what they're thinking. You should focus on the writers' attitudes to <u>education</u>, not anything else.

2) The question asks you to <u>compare</u>, so you need to write about the <u>similarities</u> and <u>differences</u> between the writers' attitudes, and <u>link</u> them together using words and phrases such as 'however' and 'in contrast'.

3) There are two bullet points to guide you. Read them <u>carefully</u> and cover what they <u>ask for</u> in your answer.

* You need to identify what the writers's <u>attitudes</u> to <u>education</u> are, and clearly <u>compare</u> them.
* You also need to compare <u>how</u> the writers have shown their attitudes to education, i.e. the <u>words</u>, <u>phrases</u> and <u>language techniques</u> they've used.

4) Support each point with relevant <u>evidence</u> from the text — using <u>short quotations</u> is a great way to do this.

Here's a **Grade 4-5** answer extract

This answer starts with a good comparison point.

Rishi Sunak believes that rural schools should be given more money, whereas Lawton B. Evans believes that it is not money but attention that rural schools need. For example, Sunak says that schools should all receive their "fair share" of funding, but that currently many schools are "under-funded". He repeats the idea of "fair share", which shows how important he thinks it is.

This is good — it picks up on a technique that the writer uses and comments on how it is used to convey the writer's point of view.

In contrast, Lawton B. Evans is fixed on the idea that people's "thought" and "study" has been focused on schools in the city for too long, but he doesn't mention money. He thinks that people in rural areas could "live more comfortably and more happily", and that education can help them achieve this. This shows that he thinks it's important to pay more attention to education because it can improve the lives of people living in rural communities.

This is a good point, but it needs more explanation of <u>how</u> the writer conveys their argument.

1) This answer starts to explore the writers' <u>attitudes</u> and begins to comment on how <u>language</u> and <u>structure</u> are used to <u>show</u> those attitudes.

2) However, it could go into more detail by using more <u>examples</u>, and explaining them more <u>clearly</u> and <u>accurately</u>.

Graded Answers — Section A, Question 6

Here's a **Grade 6-7** answer extract

Both writers say that education is an important part of society. In the newspaper article by Rishi Sunak, the text is structured so that **the same idea is repeated at the beginning and end of the article**: that education is the "greatest single tool" that can allow you to "change" your "life". By presenting this idea at the beginning and end of the article, Sunak emphasises how important he feels it is: he clearly wants the reader to remember what he is saying.

Lawton B. Evans also uses the structure of his article to convey the idea that education is an important part of society. For example, in the third paragraph he uses **repetition, starting several sentences in a row with the phrase "We need".** The use of the verb "need" in this phrase emphasises that a good-quality education is not just desirable, but necessary for all members of society. The concepts he introduces, such as "skilled" labour and "intelligent" farm management, show the reader that there are many positive effects of education, which encourages them to agree with **Evans's idea that better education in rural areas will have a positive impact on local communities.**

'Cyclical' would have been a better technical term to describe this structure.

This answer clearly compares how the two writers get across their arguments.

This answer consistently covers the bullet points — what the writers' attitudes are and how they're conveyed — and good quotes are used to back up each point.

This answer could be improved by comparing the writers' techniques in more detail...

This is a **Grade 8-9** answer extract

Both writers are attempting to persuade their respective readerships that there are flaws in the current educational system; to do this, they both use an **assured tone** that suggests the factual, reliable nature of the information they are presenting to the reader.

Rishi Sunak creates this tone using a variety of examples and statistics, which underline the injustice he perceives in the education system. For example, he describes how a pupil in "one of the top five funded areas" in the country receives "£2,000 more" than pupils in North Yorkshire. This statistic suggests that Sunak's stance is well-researched and grounded in reality, which helps to contribute to the overall confident tone in the article.

Lawton B. Evans, **on the other hand,** does not include statistical evidence; nevertheless, his choice of language means that his article has a **similar tone to Rishi Sunak's.** He explains that rural residents, when educated, "will accomplish as much as now in far less time", and "will live more comfortably and more happily". In phrases such as these, **the verb "will" emphasises Evans's certainty about the effects of improving education in rural areas, creating a general tone of confidence that strengthens his argument** and mirrors the tone of Sunak's article.

This starts by clearly comparing the purpose of both texts, then goes on to write about the methods that the writers use.

These phrases show that you're continuously comparing the two writers.

This is a good, detailed analysis of how the writer's language conveys their argument.

This answer is really good — it makes a clear, sustained comparison of the writers' views, and it discusses in depth how each writer conveys their ideas.

Graded Answers — Section B

This is the first of the two section B writing questions. These pages include some sample answers for it.

Here's the **First Writing Question**

The bullet points for this question give you some things to include in your answer. Take a look at them on p.99.

2	1	Your school wants to encourage students to take up more outdoor hobbies.
		Write a report for the school governors suggesting ways this might be done. [20 marks]

This question asks you to **Advise** and **Inform** the reader

1) The first question in section B asks you to give the reader some <u>information</u> and then <u>advise</u> them.

2) You need to match your writing to the <u>form</u>, <u>purpose</u> and <u>audience</u> you've been given in the question.

- The <u>form</u> is a <u>report</u> — so you could use an <u>impersonal</u>, <u>objective</u> tone to convey your ideas.
- The <u>purpose</u> is to <u>inform</u> and <u>advise</u>, so you need a <u>logical</u> structure to your answer, with a clear <u>introduction</u> and <u>conclusion</u>.
- The <u>audience</u> is your <u>school governors</u> — you need to appeal to an <u>unfamiliar</u>, <u>adult</u> audience.

There's some advice on how to write a report on p.76.

3) Don't forget there are 8 marks on offer for <u>spelling</u>, <u>punctuation</u> and <u>grammar</u> for this question, so it's really important to write <u>accurately</u> and <u>clearly</u>, with a good range of <u>vocabulary</u> (see p.9-10).

Here's a **Grade 4-5** answer extract

> This report suggests that the school sets up several extra-curricular clubs, which will help to encourage students to take up outdoor hobbies. Examples could include **traditional clubs such as tennis, football, hockey and netball, or unusual options such as bird-watching or mountain climbing.** The unusual options will be less familiar to students, which might make them seem more exciting or appealing. Offering a range of different activities will be key to the success of this plan.
>
> To persuade students to take up these hobbies, it would be a good idea to advertise them through the school, including in the newsletter and in school assemblies. If teachers are enthusiastic enough and they make the benefits of outdoor activities clear, then students will surely be persuaded to take part. **This will lead to a healthier, happier and more active school population.**
>
> The school could also offer residential school trips, such as camping. **These can be a nightmare to organise**, but they are exciting for students and will encourage them to continue doing outdoor activities after the trip is over. They also provide an opportunity for students to make friends, which **was** an added bonus for the overall happiness and harmony of the school.

For a report, it would be better to start with a clear introductory paragraph instead of just one sentence.

This is a good range of ideas for activities that students might enjoy, and it responds clearly to one of the bullet points in the question.

This isn't relevant to the question.

This is a bit informal — it's not really appropriate for the audience or form.

This doesn't quite make sense — the wrong tense has been used. This would lose you marks for technical accuracy.

1) This answer clearly responds to the <u>bullet points</u> in the question by suggesting outdoor hobby <u>ideas</u> and exploring ways to <u>persuade</u> students.

2) However, the <u>structure</u> isn't very sophisticated, and the language could be more <u>interesting</u> and <u>complex</u>.

Graded Answers — Section B

The following report outlines the best ways to encourage students to take up a wider variety of outdoor hobbies. **This report contains suggestions for activities in which** **students might wish to participate, and also offers some suggestions regarding how** **the school might go about persuading reluctant students to take part.**

Having closely considered the options, this report has concluded that most teenagers prefer to take part in activities that are more unusual or exciting than the norm. As such, activities such as rowing or hiking **are likely to be more popular than** commonplace activities such as athletics or ball games. It is useful to bear these preferences in mind when appealing to students to take up a new activity.

It can be difficult to persuade students to start doing outdoor activities. This report recommends making use of all the options available to the school; in particular, PE lessons could be used as a means of introducing students to a variety of enjoyable activities that they might wish to take up on a regular basis at a later date.

This answer responds to the bullet points in a way that's appropriate for the form.

A confident, assured tone is appropriate when writing to inform and advise.

This answer is clearly structured using paragraphs, but they could be more fluently linked together.

1) This answer is <u>well suited</u> to the form, purpose and audience given in the question, and it covers the <u>bullet points</u> clearly.

2) It could be improved by having a more imaginative <u>structure</u> and by using more interesting <u>language</u>.

This report explores possible ways that Dynor Secondary School could encourage greater **participation in outdoor hobbies,** as raised by the school governors at a PTA meeting on Wednesday 7th December. At the meeting it was concluded that the school would like to play a more active role in encouraging outdoor hobbies; this report explores possibilities in this regard, as well as offering suggestions for **accessible outdoor hobbies** that students might enjoy.

Access is perhaps the greatest barrier for students at Dynor Secondary School; as an urban school, hobbies such as hiking or climbing are often impractical. **It is therefore** **suggested** that the school focus its energies on promoting outdoor activities that are appropriate for an urban environment. From research conducted within the local community, it has been determined that these are likely to consist of group sports activities, such as football, basketball and hockey. **Given the sociable nature of most outdoor sports games,** **it is hoped that students will require minimal persuasion to take part; nevertheless, the** **remainder of this report will present some ideas for increased participation, making full** **use of the channels of promotion available within Dynor Secondary School.**

This opening sentence makes it clear what the report will be about.

This is a nice, subtle way to link two paragraphs together.

Formal language like this is appropriate for an informative report.

Complex sentence structures like this will impress the examiner.

This is a great answer — it's appropriate for the <u>form</u>, <u>purpose</u> and <u>audience</u>, and it uses complex, interesting <u>language</u> and <u>sentence structures</u>.

Graded Answers — Section B

You need to answer both questions in section B. Here are some sample answers for the second question.

Here is a reminder of the Second Writing Question

| 2 2 | Your local council wants to encourage young people to have part-time jobs before the age of sixteen. |

You are going to write an article for a broadsheet newspaper to share your views on this idea. You could agree or disagree with the council's idea.

Write an engaging article for a broadsheet newspaper giving your views.   **[20 marks]**

Adapt your Writing Style to the question

It doesn't matter what your opinion is, as long as your answer is engaging and well-structured.

1) The second question in section B asks for your <u>own perspective</u> on the council's idea to encourage people under the age of 16 to have part-time jobs.

2) You need to match your writing to the <u>form</u>, <u>purpose</u> and <u>audience</u> you've been given in the question.

- The <u>form</u> is a broadsheet newspaper article, so you could write an <u>opinion piece</u> (see pages 71-73).

- The <u>purpose</u> is to <u>explain</u> your point of view, which you could do by making an <u>argument</u> for your viewpoint.

- The <u>audience</u> isn't mentioned specifically, but it's a broadsheet newspaper article about working under the age of 16, so it's likely to be read by <u>adults</u> who have <u>children</u> of around that age.

3) Think about <u>structure</u> too — especially the <u>opening</u>, <u>ending</u>, and how to <u>link</u> your paragraphs together.

4) Don't forget there are 8 marks on offer for <u>spelling</u>, <u>punctuation</u> and <u>grammar</u> for this question — it's really important to write <u>accurately</u> and <u>clearly</u> with a good range of <u>vocabulary</u> (see p.9-10).

Here's a Grade 4-5 answer extract

This answer uses a counter-argument to strengthen the point it's making.

A new paragraph should start here.

This opening sentence isn't really appropriate for a broadsheet newspaper.

The repetition of rhetorical questions is a nice language feature here — it makes the point of view come across more forcefully.

NO PART-TIME JOBS FOR UNDER-SIXTEENS

I think that children under the age of 16 shouldn't get a part-time job. Although some people might argue that having a job teaches children about the value of money, time management and working as a team, I don't think that this is the case.

Firstly, most children already have good time management skills. Schools start at 9 am, and some even earlier than this, so arriving on time to lessons is already second nature to most children. Why should children have a part-time job when they already know how to manage their time? Secondly, most children have been working as a team since primary school. From sports teams in P.E., to group projects in Science, school teaches children how to work together from a very young age. Why should children give up their weekends for a badly paid job when they already have great teamwork skills?

1) This answer makes some <u>good points</u> that are focused on the <u>question</u>.

2) It could be better matched to the <u>form</u> — the <u>tone</u> and <u>style</u> don't always fit a <u>broadsheet newspaper</u>.

3) The language could be more varied — including <u>humour</u> or more <u>creative vocabulary</u> would gain marks.

Graded Answers — Section B

Here's a **Grade 6-7** answer extract

SAVE THE LEARNING FOR THE CLASSROOM

Lots of young people have a part-time job, and I am sure that employment teaches them a whole host of valuable skills: communication, time management and independence to name but a few. However, these skills aren't just learnt in the workplace; many young people develop and refine these skills in the classroom.

Take, for instance, communication. Every day in school, pupils communicate with a wide range of people. Pupils learn to talk respectfully to teachers; they learn how to make engaging conversation with their friends; and they learn how to communicate their ideas effectively to their peers during group work. **School doesn't just allow pupils to practise their verbal communication — it allows them to develop their written communication too.** Essays teach students how to summarise their thoughts, and present their opinions. What part-time job could develop communication more effectively than this?

The answer uses sophisticated punctuation accurately.

The tone of this answer is suitable for the form and purpose. It's a bit more chatty than the previous answer, but it still uses good vocabulary.

The ideas are linked together fluently.

1) This answer uses language techniques, a <u>clear structure</u> and <u>creative vocabulary</u> to get its point across.

2) However, if the author's <u>personality</u> came across more strongly, the text would be more <u>compelling</u>.

Here's a **Grade 8-9** answer extract

A headline and strapline are used to grab the reader's attention.

MINIMUM WAGE, MINIMUM GAIN

Part-time jobs have little value for teenagers under sixteen, argues Charlie Lin.

If someone were to ask me whether I thought under-sixteens should get part-time jobs, my answer, **unequivocally**, would be "no". **As I write this, I can imagine the shocked looks on my readers' faces** and the **disdainful** cries of "but employment teaches children valuable life skills!" To these critics, I say this: there's nothing a part-time job can teach children that they can't learn from other, more rewarding options.

If you don't believe me, then think about the jobs that are actually available to under-sixteens. Paper rounds, waiting tables, shop assistant — essentially an assortment of mundane, badly-paid Saturday jobs. And what 'valuable life skills' might they learn while toiling away for less than minimum wage? "Teamwork!" you might cry triumphantly, "working in a cafe would teach a young person how to work as part of a team." **This may certainly be true if you believe being belittled by the chef and bossed around by the manager counts as 'teamwork'.** I, however, do not. If that same child was part of a football team, working alongside their peers, practising hard to achieve a common goal (annihilating the rival team), now that would be teamwork.

Really interesting and varied vocabulary makes this answer high-level.

Lots of rhetorical techniques are used in this paragraph to make the writer's point of view clear and their argument compelling.

The writer shows a clear awareness of their audience.

A sarcastic tone makes the argument convincingly, but also gives a sense of the writer's personality.

The writer's <u>opinion</u> and <u>personality</u> is clear in this answer, and it's <u>fluently written</u>. The tone is humorous and chatty, but also subtle, which makes the answer <u>engaging</u> and <u>readable</u>.

As final preparation, here are some <u>practice papers</u> to test how well-prepared you are for the real thing.

- There are <u>two</u> practice papers:
  Component 1: 20th Century Literature Reading and Creative Prose Writing (pages 116-119)
  Component 2: 19th and 21st Century Non-Fiction Reading and Transactional/Persuasive Writing (pages 120-124)

- Before you start each paper, read through all the <u>instructions</u>, <u>information</u> and <u>advice</u> on the front.

- You'll need some paper to write your answers on.

- When you've finished, have a look at the answers starting on page 125 — they'll give you some ideas of the kind of things you should have included in your answers.

- <u>Don't</u> try to do both of the papers in one sitting.

CGP Practice Exam Paper
GCSE English Language

General Certificate of Secondary Education

GCSE
English Language – Component 1

20th Century Literature Reading and Creative Prose Writing

Time allowed: 1 hour 45 minutes

Centre name					
Centre number					
Candidate number					

Surname
Other names
Candidate signature

Instructions to candidates
- Write your answers in **black** ink or ball-point pen.
- Answer **all** questions in Section A.
- Select **one** title to write about in Section B.
- Write your name and other details in the boxes above.

Information for candidates
- The marks available are given in brackets at the end of each question.
- There are 80 marks available for this exam paper.

Advice for candidates
- You should spend your time as follows:
  Section A — about 10 minutes reading through the sources and all five questions
             about 50 minutes answering the questions
  Section B — about 10 minutes planning
             about 35 minutes writing

This extract is the opening of a short story set in New Zealand, written in 1922 by Katherine Mansfield.

At the Bay

Very early morning. The sun was not yet risen, and the whole of Crescent Bay was hidden under a white sea-mist. The big bush-covered hills at the back were smothered. You could not see where they ended and the paddocks and bungalows began. The sandy road was gone and the paddocks and bungalows the other side of it; there were no white dunes covered with reddish grass beyond them;
5 there was nothing to mark which was beach and where was the sea. A heavy dew had fallen. The grass was blue. Big drops hung on the bushes and just did not fall; the silvery, fluffy toi-toi* was limp on its long stalks, and all the marigolds and the pinks in the bungalow gardens were bowed to the earth with wetness. Drenched were the cold fuchsias, round pearls of dew lay on the flat nasturtium leaves. It looked as though the sea had beaten up softly in the darkness, as though one immense wave had
10 come rippling, rippling — how far? Perhaps if you had waked up in the middle of the night you might have seen a big fish flicking in at the window and gone again...

Ah-Aah! sounded the sleepy sea. And from the bush there came the sound of little streams flowing, quickly, lightly, slipping between the smooth stones, gushing into ferny basins and out again; and there was the splashing of big drops on large leaves, and something else — what was it? — a faint stirring and
15 shaking, the snapping of a twig and then such silence that it seemed some one was listening.

Round the corner of Crescent Bay, between the piled-up masses of broken rock, a flock of sheep came pattering. They were huddled together, a small, tossing, woolly mass, and their thin, stick-like legs trotted along quickly as if the cold and the quiet had frightened them. Behind them an old sheep-dog, his soaking paws covered with sand, ran along with his nose to the ground, but carelessly,
20 as if thinking of something else. And then in the rocky gateway the shepherd himself appeared. He was a lean, upright old man, in a frieze** coat that was covered with a web of tiny drops, velvet trousers tied under the knee, and a wide-awake*** with a folded blue handkerchief round the brim.

One hand was crammed into his belt, the other grasped a beautifully smooth yellow stick. And as he walked, taking his time, he kept up a very soft light whistling, an airy, far-away fluting that sounded
25 mournful and tender. The old dog cut an ancient caper or two and then drew up sharp, ashamed of his levity, and walked a few dignified paces by his master's side. The sheep ran forward in little pattering rushes; they began to bleat, and ghostly flocks and herds answered them from under the sea. "Baa! Baaa!" For a time they seemed to be always on the same piece of ground.

There ahead was stretched the sandy road with shallow puddles; the same soaking bushes showed
30 on either side and the same shadowy palings****. Then something immense came into view; an enormous shock-haired giant with his arms stretched out. It was the big gum-tree outside Mrs. Stubbs' shop, and as they passed by there was a strong whiff of eucalyptus. And now big spots of light gleamed in the mist. The shepherd stopped whistling; he rubbed his red nose and wet beard on his wet sleeve and, screwing up his eyes, glanced in the direction of the sea. The sun was rising. It was marvellous
35 how quickly the mist thinned, sped away, dissolved from the shallow plain, rolled up from the bush and was gone as if in a hurry to escape; big twists and curls jostled and shouldered each other as the silvery beams broadened. The far-away sky — a bright, pure blue — was reflected in the puddles, and the drops, swimming along the telegraph poles, flashed into points of light. Now the leaping, glittering sea was so bright it made one's eyes ache to look at it. The shepherd drew a pipe, the bowl as small as an
40 acorn, out of his breast pocket, fumbled for a chunk of speckled tobacco, pared off a few shavings and stuffed the bowl. He was a grave, fine-looking old man. As he lit up and the blue smoke wreathed his head, the dog, watching, looked proud of him.

"Baa! Baaa!" The sheep spread out into a fan. They were just clear of the summer colony before the first sleeper turned over and lifted a drowsy head; their cry sounded in the dreams of little
45 children... who lifted their arms to drag down, to cuddle the darling little woolly lambs of sleep. Then

the first inhabitant appeared; it was the Burnells' cat Florrie, sitting on the gatepost, far too early as usual, looking for their milk-girl. When she saw the old sheep-dog she sprang up quickly, arched her back, drew in her tabby head, and seemed to give a little fastidious shiver. "Ugh! What a coarse, revolting creature!" said Florrie. But the old sheep-dog, not looking up, waggled past, flinging out his
50 legs from side to side. Only one of his ears twitched to prove that he saw, and thought her a silly young female. The breeze of morning lifted in the bush and the smell of leaves and wet black earth mingled with the sharp smell of the sea. Myriads of birds were singing. A goldfinch flew over the shepherd's head and, perching on the tiptop of a spray, it turned to the sun, ruffling its small breast feathers. And now they had passed the fisherman's hut, passed the charred-looking little whare***** where Leila the
55 milk-girl lived with her old Gran. The sheep strayed over a yellow swamp and Wag, the sheep-dog, padded after, rounded them up and headed them for the steeper, narrower rocky pass that led out of Crescent Bay and towards Daylight Cove. "Baa! Baa!" Faint the cry came as they rocked along the fast-drying road. The shepherd put away his pipe, dropping it into his breast-pocket so that the little bowl hung over. And straightway the soft airy whistling began again. Wag ran out along a ledge of
60 rock after something that smelled, and ran back again disgusted. Then pushing, nudging, hurrying, the sheep rounded the bend and the shepherd followed after out of sight.

Glossary

*	toi-toi — a type of tall grass
**	frieze — coarse woollen cloth
***	wide-awake — a type of wide-brimmed hat
****	palings — pointed fence-posts
*****	whare — a hut

Section A: Reading

*Answer **all** the questions in this section.*

0	1	**Read lines 1-8.**

List **five** things you learn about Crescent Bay from these lines.

(5 marks)

0	2	**Read lines 9-15.**

How does the writer show what Crescent Bay looks and sounds like?

You must refer to the text to support your answer, using relevant subject terminology.

(5 marks)

0	3	**Read lines 16-28.**

What impressions do you get of the shepherd and the animals from these lines?

You must refer to the language used in the text to support your answer, using relevant subject terminology.

(10 marks)

0 4 **Read lines 29-42.**

How does the writer make these lines vivid and interesting?

You should write about:

- the writer's use of language to make these lines vivid and interesting;
- how the structure of these lines makes them vivid and interesting;
- the effects on the reader.

You must refer to the text to support your answer, using relevant subject terminology.

(10 marks)

0 5 **Read lines 43 to the end.**

"In the last twenty or so lines of this passage, the writer is successful in creating a believable scene and set of characters for the reader."

To what extent do you agree with this view?

You should write about:

- your own impressions of the scene and the characters, both here and in the passage as a whole;
- how the writer has created these impressions.

You must refer to the text to support your answer.

(10 marks)

Section B: Writing

*In this section you will be assessed for the quality of your **creative prose writing** skills.*

24 marks are awarded for communication and organisation.

16 marks are awarded for vocabulary, sentence structure, spelling and punctuation.

You should aim to write about 450-600 words.

1 1 Choose **one** of the following titles for your writing:

Either, (a) The Journey.

Or, (b) The Misty Morning.

Or, (c) Write about a time when you went for a walk.

Or, (d) Write a story which begins:
After all these years, who would have thought that...

(40 marks)

General Certificate of Secondary Education

GCSE
English Language – Component 2
19th and 21st Century Non-Fiction Reading and Transactional/Persuasive Writing

Time allowed: 2 hours

Centre name					
Centre number					
Candidate number					

Surname
Other names
Candidate signature

Instructions to candidates
- Write your answers in **black** ink or ball-point pen.
- Answer **all** the questions.
- Write your name and other details in the boxes above.

Information for candidates
- The marks available are given in brackets at the end of each question.
- There are 80 marks available for this exam paper.

Advice for candidates
- You should spend your time as follows:
  Section A — about 10 minutes reading through the sources and all six questions
          about 50 minutes answering the questions
  Section B — about 30 minutes on each question (5 minutes planning and 25 minutes reading)

21st-Century Source

The following text is an extract from an article in a broadsheet newspaper
by a journalist called Jenni Russell. It was published in 2005.

What are friends for?

Earlier this year, I rang my friend Jo and found her in a state of stunned misery.

Jo is a witty, sexy, single, childless woman in her 40s. She's a talented artist, but earns very little. Without a career, money, husband or family to bolster her confidence, a small group of friends have been a key part of her identity. Genevieve, an ambitious, glamorous woman whom she met at
5   university, has been her constant confidante* for almost a quarter of a century. But in the past three or four years, Genevieve has become increasingly unreliable: making dates she later cancels; slow to return calls or emails.

Last winter, Jo arranged for them to go to a film together, only for Genevieve to ring at 6pm to say she was awfully sorry, but she had to spend the evening with some dreary Burmese** refugees, friends
10   of her father's. Fortunately for Jo, 20 minutes later she was rung and asked to make up the numbers for a formal dinner party. When she walked into the room, she felt as if she had been punched in the stomach. Genevieve was sitting on the sofa, flirting with the men on either side of her. There were no refugees.

"The next day I sent her an email saying: 'Why did you lie to me? Why not just say: I want to go to
15   a dinner party? I can take that. I can't take being lied to. This is a friendship. We're supposed to trust one another.' She emailed back immediately saying she didn't have to explain herself to me. And then a month later she said our friendship had run its course, and she wouldn't be seeing me any more. It's one of the worst things that's ever happened to me. And I haven't just lost her; I've lost all our history, all that shared experience."

20   Often, we don't know where we fit into friends' lives. Are we in the first dozen, or the remotest 90 in their circle? If they ask us to dinner once a year, is that an honour because they only entertain twice, or a sign of our unimportance, because they hold dinners every week?

This degree of uncertainty exists partly because many of us now lead lives in which we are the only connecting thread. It is perfectly possible for much of our lives to be opaque to anyone who knows us.
25   They may only ever encounter one particular facet of our existence, because we can, if we choose, keep parents, past acquaintances, old partners, colleagues, friends, and neighbours in totally separate boxes. Many people value the anonymity and freedom that gives them. The flip side is that just as we are not known, so we cannot really know others.

Talking to a wide range of people, it was clear that few of them are really happy with the friendships
30   they have. People with consuming jobs are sad that they haven't had the time to build stronger bonds, and wonder whether it's too late to develop them; mothers with time to spare want to find new friends but don't know how. Many people would like to have more friends, or deeper, warmer, more reliable relationships than the ones they have now, but don't know how to go about it.

There are powerful reasons why we should create these bonds, even if we only start when we are
35   older. The phenomenon of later births means families take up a smaller percentage of our lives. We wait years to have children, and we could be 70 before we become grandparents for the first time. We have more time available, and fewer familial responsibilities, than the generations before us. We all want to feel needed and valued by others. It is possible for friends to fill that need, but only if we work at it.

40   It isn't easy, because friendship is a subtle dance, and no one wants to be explicitly pursued when it's unwelcome, or explicitly dropped when they are not wanted. Nor does it come with any guarantees. People are unpredictable. But we need to play the game of friendship. Evidence shows that people with close friends live longer and are happier than those without. And friendship defines what it means to be human.

19th-Century Source

This is an extract from a piece by Wilkie Collins, which appeared in a periodical called 'Household Words' in 1858. A periodical was a collection of fiction and non-fiction that related to the topics of the day, published once a week or once a month (similar to a modern magazine). Collins has just described a beggar addressing a crowd in the street — this extract starts with his report of the beggar's speech.

Save me from my friends

"Good Christian people, will you be so obliging as to leave off your various occupations for a few minutes only, and listen to the harrowing statement of a father of a family, who is reduced to acknowledge his misfortunes in the public streets? Work, honest work, is all I ask for; and I cannot get it. Good Christian people, I think it is because I have no friends. Must I perish in a land of plenty because I have
5   no work and because I have no friends?"

"No friends!" I repeated to myself, as I walked away. But can the marvellous assertion be true? Can this enviable man really go home and touch up his speech for to-morrow, with the certainty of not being interrupted? I am going home to finish an article, without knowing whether I shall have a clear five minutes to myself, all the time I am at work. Can he take his money back to his drawer, in broad daylight,
10   and meet nobody by the way who will say to him, 'Remember our old friendship, and lend me a trifle'? I have money waiting for me at my publisher's, and I dare not go to fetch it, except under cover of the night. No wonder that he looks prosperous and healthy, though he lives in a dingy slum, and that I look peevish and pale, though I reside on gravel, in an airy neighbourhood.

It is a dreadful thing to say (even anonymously); but it is the sad truth that I could positively dispense
15   with a great many of my dearest friends.

There is my Boisterous Friend, for instance. I always know when he calls, though my study is at the top of the house. I hear him in the passage, the moment the door is opened. I have told my servant to say that I am engaged, which means simply, that I am hard at work. "Dear old boy!" I hear my Boisterous Friend exclaim, with a genial roar, "writing away, the jolly, hard-working, clever old chap, just as usual —
20   eh, Susan? Lord bless you! he knows me — he knows I don't want to interrupt him." My door is burst open, as if with a battering-ram (no boisterous man ever knocks), and my friend rushes in like a mad bull. "Ha, ha, ha! I've caught you," says the associate of my childhood. "Don't stop for me, dear old boy; I'm not going to interrupt you (Lord bless my soul, what a lot of writing!) — and you're all right, eh? No! I won't sit down; I won't stop another instant. So glad to have seen you dear fellow — good bye." By this
25   time, his affectionate voice has made the room ring again; he has squeezed my hand, in his brotherly way, till my fingers are too sore to hold the pen; and he has put to flight, for the rest of the day, every idea that I had when I sat down to work. Could I really dispense with him? I don't deny that he has known me from the time when I was in short frocks*, and that he loves me like a brother. Nevertheless, I could dispense — yes, I could dispense — oh, yes, I could dispense — with my Boisterous Friend.

30   I have not by any means done yet with the number of my dear friends whom I could dispense with. To say nothing of my friend who borrows money of me (an obvious nuisance), there is my self-satisfied friend, who can talk of nothing but himself, and his successes in life; there is my inattentive friend, who is perpetually asking me irrelevant questions, and who has no power of listening to my answers; there is my hospitable friend, who is continually telling me that he wants so much to ask me to dinner, and who never
35   does really ask me by any chance.

A double knock at the street door stops my pen suddenly. A well-known voice in the passage smites my ear, inquiring for me, on very particular business, and asking the servant to take in the name. This is my friend who does not at all like the state of my health. Well, well, I have made my confession, and eased my mind. Show him in, Susan — show him in.

Glossary

*   short frocks — the short dresses that very young children (both male and female) often wore

Section A: Reading

*Answer **all** of the following questions.*

**To answer the following questions you will need to refer
to the newspaper article by Jenni Russell on page 121.**

1	1

    (a) Where did Jo and Genevieve first meet each other? *(1 mark)*

    (b) What time did Genevieve ring to cancel the film? *(1 mark)*

    (c) According to the text, how old might some people
        be before they become grandparents? *(1 mark)*

1	2

Jenni Russell is trying to persuade us that friends are important.
How does she try to do this?

You should comment on:

• what she says to influence readers;

• her use of language, tone and structure. *(10 marks)*

**To answer the following questions you will need to refer
to the extract by Wilkie Collins on page 122.**

1	3

    (a) Why does the beggar think he can't find work? *(1 mark)*

    (b) Why will Wilkie Collins only collect
        money from his publisher's at night? *(1 mark)*

    (c) What is the name of Wilkie Collins's servant? *(1 mark)*

1	4

What do you think and feel about Wilkie Collins's views on his Boisterous Friend?

You should comment on:

• what is said;

• how it is said.

You must refer to the text to support your comments. *(10 marks)*

To answer the following questions you will need to use both texts.

1	5

According to these two writers, why can relationships with other people
be problematic? *(4 marks)*

1	6

Both of these texts are about friendship. Compare the following:

• the writers' attitudes to friendship;

• how they get across their views.

*You must use the text to support your comments and make it clear
which text you are referring to.* *(10 marks)*

Section B: Writing

*Answer **both** questions.*

In this section you will be assessed for the quality of your writing skills.

For each question, 12 marks are awarded for communication and organisation;
8 marks are awarded for vocabulary, sentence structure, punctuation and spelling.

Think about the purpose and audience for your writing.

You should aim to write about 300-400 words for each task.

2 1 Your headteacher is keen to ensure that new students at your school are able to settle in and make friends.

Write a letter to the headteacher suggesting ways this could be done.

You could include:

• examples of the difficulties that new students encounter;

• your ideas about things that could be done to help new students. *(20 marks)*

2 2 A proposal has been made to make studying one foreign language compulsory up until the age of 18.

You have been asked to write an article about the proposal from a student's perspective, to be published in a broadsheet newspaper. You could write in favour or against this proposal.

Write a lively article for the newspaper giving your views. *(20 marks)*

Page 20 — Warm-Up Questions

1) a) True
   b) False

2) a) Rita
   b) Rita
   c) Rakesh
   d) E.g. "bad enough that we have to go to this reunion at all"
      E.g. "Rita glared pointedly at her watch"
      E.g. "admiring his reflection"

3) a) Adults. E.g. 'because the writer uses complex language like "yearn" and the subject matter doesn't apply to children'.
   b) Novices. E.g. 'because the writer uses simple, general explanations which suggests it's written for people who have never bought a used car before'.

4) a) To advise. E.g. 'because the writer uses simple language that the reader will understand to suggest what the reader should do'.
   b) To entertain. E.g. 'because the writer uses descriptive verbs such as "crawling" and "gallop" to engage the reader'.
   c) To persuade. E.g. 'because the writer uses a rhetorical question to encourage the reader to agree with their argument'.

Pages 21-22 — Exam-Style Questions

1) Any five correct facts about George, either paraphrased or directly quoted from the text. For example:
   • George has a nasal voice.
   • George has a loud voice.
   • George is wearing a "garish purple suit".
   • George has an "elaborate hairstyle".
   • George brings a bottle of wine to the party.
   • George has "greasy" hands.
   • George is wearing several rings.
   • George likes whisky.

2) Answers should use relevant quotes or examples from both texts to clearly answer the question. Here are some things you could mention:
   • People should read because it can entertain for long periods of time. The 19th-century writer says that they can read for "hours and hours", and the 21st-century text says that you can read for "hours on end".
   • People should read because it is educational. The 19th-century writer says that they have learnt about "fascinating places" from books, and the 21st-century writer says that books have widened their "horizons".

3) a) a fortnight
   b) to stay out of the rain
   c) archery

4) All your points should use relevant examples and terminology, and comment on the effects of the language, tone and structure. Here are some things you could mention:
   • Casual style to make the reader comfortable, e.g. "Unless you've been living under a rock for the past month".
   • Use of the imperative form ("don't panic", "have a look") to give clear guidance to the reader.
   • Introductory/concluding paragraphs create a clear structure and summarise the information to make it easier for the reader to understand.

Page 30 — Exam-Style Questions

1) Answers should clearly compare the different ideas and techniques in each text, using quotations to support points. Here are some things you could mention:
   • In the 19th-century letter, the writer illustrates their dislike of a new art style using hyperbole ("nothing short of an abomination"). In the 21st-century newspaper article, the writer expresses their admiration for a new art style, also using hyperbole ("They're revolutionaries").
   • Both texts use formal language, e.g. "I read with concern" in the 19th-century letter, "progression in the medium" in the 21st-century newspaper article. This makes their opinion seem more important / authoritative.
   • The 21st-century writer makes the restrictions of traditional art seem negative using a metaphor, "the iron shackles of 'traditional art'", whereas the writer of the 19th-century letter thinks that the rules of traditional art are good: new artists should have "learnt from" older examples.

2) Your answer should evaluate the text by offering an opinion on the statement. It should comment on the techniques used to describe both characters, using relevant examples and terminology to support each point. Here are some things you could mention:
   • I agree that you can identify with both characters, because dialogue is used to give an insight into each character's mindset, such as Annie: "Don't be ridiculous." and Lucas: "They'll kill me." This indicates that Annie is calmer and less prone to being overdramatic in comparison to Lucas.
   • The cumulative use of short sentences in Lucas's speech also emphasises his stress and helps the reader to identify with his panic, e.g. "I've looked everywhere. It's lost. They'll kill me."
   • The contrast between the two characters makes each character's personality stand out more and their individual perspective seem clearer. E.g. the adjectives used to describe Lucas's actions ("frantic", "manic") contrast with the adverbs used to describe Annie's actions, which are carried out "cautiously" or "calmly".

Page 36 — Warm-Up Questions

1) a) Detached
   b) Upbeat
   c) Sentimental

2) Sentence a)

3) E.g. 'The tone is conversational. The writer uses slang phrases such as "cheesed off", and contractions like "it's", as well as humour when describing the trip to "River C and Swamp D".'

4) a) E.g. 'Customers are advised that we do not accept credit cards.'
   b) E.g. 'It is essential to ensure you have the correct tools before proceeding.'

5) Noun: Bella   Verb: approached   Adverb: excitedly

6) E.g. 'The word "whispered" suggests that the speaker and listener are working together, whilst "spat" suggests that the speaker doesn't like the listener.'

7) a) ii) money
   b) E.g. 'It suggests that the narrator is very motivated by money. They see their sibling's theatre show as an opportunity to "cash in" and talk about time as something you can "buy".'

8) E.g. 'The verbs are very violent, which creates the impression that the wind is powerful and destructive.'

Page 37 — Exam-Style Questions

1) All your points should use relevant examples and terminology, and comment on the effects of the language used. Here are some things you could mention:
- The repetition of the word 'wind' — "a bitter wind, a stinging wind, a wind that drowned..." — to emphasise the overwhelming nature of the wind.
- Words and phrases that indicate noise: "roaring cacophony", "howling", "roar", to appeal to the reader's senses and make the storm more vivid.
- Violent verbs, such as "barged", "wrenched" and "savaged", to emphasise that the storm is destructive.

2) All your points should use relevant examples and terminology, and comment on the effects of the language used and its influence on the reader. Here are some things you could mention:
- Words and phrases associated with cold emphasise the woman's detached personality ("icily", "stone cold").
- The adverb in the phrase "breath caught painfully" suggests that the man's fear is physically painful.
- The simile "like a condemned man" emphasises that the man feels resigned to his fate, and indicates that the woman is in a position of great power.

Page 47 — Warm-Up Questions

1) E.g. 'It suggests that the lake is something to be wary of.'

2) E.g. 'The second text compares the water to something that the reader is familiar with, to make it easier to visualise.'

3) a) Personification. E.g. 'It makes the computer seem like it's mocking the writer, which conveys the writer's frustration.'
   b) Onomatopoeia. E.g. 'It helps the reader to imagine the noise created by the students.'
   c) Alliteration. E.g. 'It makes the text more memorable.'

4) E.g. 'Sarcasm is nastier than irony, because it has a mocking tone that's often meant to insult someone.'

5) Yes. E.g. 'The text is sarcastic because the positive phrase "Ivan is a brilliant secretary" contrasts with the negative context "he keeps forgetting to bring a pen".'

6) a) Antithesis. E.g. 'It highlights the contrast between the writer's expectations and reality, which makes the reality seem more disappointing.'
   b) Parenthesis. E.g. 'It creates familiarity between the writer and the readers, so they are more likely to be persuaded.'
   c) Hyperbole. E.g. 'It emphasises how terrible the writer feels the rain would be.'

7) E.g. 'It gives the writer's opinion as fact ("By far the best hobby") and makes generalisations, such as claiming that all young people "adore" playing cribbage.'

8) E.g. 'The descriptive adjectives "blistering" and "prickly" suggest that the weather is physically uncomfortable. The imagery "as if I were underwater" helps the reader to imagine the physical strain on the narrator, which is furthered by the descriptive verb "trudged".'

Pages 48-49 — Exam-Style Questions

1) All your points should use relevant examples and terminology, and comment on the effects of the language used and its influence on the reader. Here are some things you could mention:
- The use of animal similes and metaphors indicate how vulnerable the workers are — "like mice in a cage", "lambs" — in contrast to the soldiers, who are "wolves".
- The use of a simile suggests the officer in charge of the prisoners has a forceful, unfriendly personality— "fired his orders like cannon balls."
- The use of the descriptive verbs "huddled" and "shivered" suggests the workers' weakness. This contrasts with the verbs "trampled" and "marched", which are used to suggest that the soldiers are powerful and authoritative.

2) All your points should use relevant examples and terminology, and comment on the effects of the language and structure used and their influence on the reader. Here are some things you could mention:
- Alliterative phrases such as "labyrinth of lost lanes" to emphasise how confusing the writer finds Kuala Lumpur.
- Personification of vehicles that "rumble past impatiently" which conveys the idea that everything in the city is animated and full of life.
- Long, complex sentences are used throughout the extract, which provide vivid and detailed description for the reader. These give a sense of being breathless, which, coupled with the mass of information they provide, highlights the overwhelming nature of Kuala Lumpur.

3) Answers should clearly compare the different attitudes and techniques in each text, using quotations to support points. Here are some things you could mention:
- The 19th-century writer has a fairly balanced viewpoint: they acknowledge positive aspects, like the room's size, as well as negative aspects, such as the "limited refreshment". This makes the writer seem more reasonable.
- The writer of the 21st-century review has a more negative viewpoint than the writer of the 19th-century letter — they instantly "doubted" that the bedding was clean, which, combined with a complete absence of positive points about the room, shows that the writer is quite biased.

4) Your answer should evaluate the text by offering an opinion on the statement. It should comment on the techniques used to describe the party, using relevant examples and terminology to support each point. Here are some things you could mention:
- The cumulative effect of using several descriptive verbs together in "joking, laughing, making introductions", to convey a sense of action and excitement to the reader.
- Onomatopoeic verbs such as "thumping" and "clinking" to help the reader to imagine what the party sounds like.
- The focus on describing colours in the third paragraph, which appeals to the senses to help the reader to visualise the upbeat mood of the party.

Page 60 — Exam-Style Questions

1) All your points should use relevant examples and terminology, and comment on the effects of the language and structure used and their influence on the reader. Here are some things you could mention:
- The shift in time that the extract uses — it starts in the present day, goes back to the past, then returns to the present. This allows the reader to become emotionally invested in Joan, so the ending has a greater impact.

- The use of sensory language, e.g. "She remembered the smell of the water", helps the reader to imagine Joan's memories clearly. This provides interest as it allows them to get to know Joan and understand her feelings, building upon the scene's emotion.
- The motif of Joan looking at the sea, which is revisited in the first and last paragraph, and is contrasted by the way she "raced into the sea" in the second paragraph. This structure adds interest to the end of the story.

2) All your points should use relevant examples and terminology, and comment on the effects of the language and structure used and their influence on the reader. Here are some things you could mention:
- Strong descriptive vocabulary such as "horrified", "dangerous" and "fatal" to convey the idea that Swampy Water is a bad product.
- Lists all of the arguments in one paragraph, linked by words like "Firstly", "Secondly" and "Finally" to give the impression that there are lots of good arguments in the writer's favour.
- Presents the opinion of the writer as fact ("clearly idiotic", "any sane parent would endorse") to make the reader think that the writer's opinion is valid.

Page 69 — Warm-Up Questions

1) b) rhetorical questions and d) emotive language

2) E.g. 'Hiding away in the sleepy village of Lyttlewich, Howtonshire, is a true gem of English architecture that you can't afford to miss. Thousands of visitors flock to the ancient Lyttlewich Church every year to marvel at its truly stunning artwork. Isn't it about time you joined the crowd?'

3) a) E.g. 'Fertilisers provide things that plants need to grow.'
   b) E.g. 'The ear bones are some of the smallest in the body.'
   c) E.g. 'Roman soldiers used weapons to defeat their enemies.'

4) a) E.g. 'Money can be tricky to get your head around, so why aren't schools teaching us how to deal with it?'
   b) E.g. 'Before you start making your yummy cake, ask an adult to help you get everything you'll need.'

5) a) E.g. 'From the diving board, the swimmers below look like a shoal of brightly coloured fish.
   b) E.g. 'The noises in the pool echo like whalesong.'
   c) E.g. 'I feel the roughness of the tiles under my bare feet.'
   d) E.g. 'The bitter chlorine catches in the back of my throat.'

6) a) E.g. 'I took a deep breath and stepped onto the alien spaceship, ready for my next adventure.'
   b) E.g. 'The familiar sounds of the river rushing outside my window were all I needed to hear; I was finally home.'

7) a) E.g. 'First person, to give an insight into the character's thoughts and feelings.'
   b) E.g. '"Eerie", to make the forest seem scary and sinister. "Timid", to make the character seem afraid.'
   c) E.g. 'The moon was shining as brightly as a new penny.'

8) Answers should include ideas for the plot and characters of a story involving a castle.

Page 70 — Exam-Style Questions

1) Answers need to be entertaining for a general, adult audience. They need to use interesting language techniques to create a suitable tone and style. Writing needs to be well-organised, clear and technically accurate. These answers are for option (c), 'Write about your local area.' Here are some techniques you could include:
- A list of adjectives: "The fields were endless, fragrant and golden in the sun's light."
- An unusual character: "The town's oldest resident, Agatha Hart, was a tiny lady who wore layers of colourful clothing that made her look at least twice her diminutive size."
- Direct address: "Perhaps you might think that nothing exciting could ever happen in a sleepy town like Drizzleford. You'd be wrong."

2) Answers need to be entertaining for a general, adult audience. They need to use interesting language techniques to create a suitable tone and style. Writing needs to be well-organised, clear and technically accurate. These answers are for option (a), 'The Penguin.' Here are some techniques you could include:
- The five senses: "The smell of fish was overwhelming. Jurgen fought down the urge to gag as he inhaled the aromas of the penguin enclosure."
- Onomatopoeia: "The penguin's wings slapped excitedly."
- A neat, satisfying ending: "The time had come; Jurgen returned the baby penguin to its mother, smiling wistfully at his memories of the fun they'd had."

3) Answers need to be entertaining for a general, adult audience. They need to use interesting language techniques to create a suitable tone and style. Writing needs to be well-organised, clear and technically accurate. These answers are for option (c), 'Write about a train journey.' Here are some techniques you could include:
- An intriguing opening: "The train that carried Steve out of the city was exactly the same as the one he'd arrived on, after that fateful day all those years ago."
- Descriptive verbs: "The train slogged and toiled its way along the tracks."
- Personification: "The houses of the city seemed to watch him reproachfully as the train sped away."

Page 82 — Exam-Style Questions

1) Answers need to reflect form, purpose and audience using suitable vocabulary and language techniques. Writing needs to be well-organised, clear and technically accurate. Here are some techniques you could include:
- Direct address: "You shouldn't spend too long staring at the screen of your tablet or smartphone."
- Imperative verbs: "Get into the habit of doing something active at least twice a week."
- Reassuring language: "It's okay if you haven't tried a sport before — most sports clubs welcome beginners."

2) Answers need to reflect form, purpose and audience using suitable vocabulary and language techniques. Writing needs to be well-organised, clear and technically accurate. Here are some techniques you could include:
- Rhetorical questions: "Do you really care about TV more than your health and wellbeing?"
- Lists of three: "The more sleep you get, the happier, healthier and brainier you'll be."
- Emotive language: "It's absolutely vital that you get enough sleep: your health and happiness depend on it."

3) Answers need to reflect form, purpose and audience using suitable vocabulary and language techniques. Writing needs to be well-organised, clear and technically accurate. Here are some techniques you could include:
- Descriptive adjectives: "We should leap at the chance to swap humdrum, drizzly British life for something new."
- First-person narrative: "In Bermuda, I saw a sunset so beautiful that it brought tears to my eyes."
- Analogy: "Trying to understand different cultures without going out and experiencing them is a little like trying to paint a portrait of something without ever seeing it: basically, you're bound to get it wrong."

4) Answers need to reflect form, purpose and audience using suitable vocabulary and language techniques. Writing needs to be well-organised, clear and technically accurate. Here are some techniques you could include:
- Formal language: "Dear sir, I write to express my concern over your article calling for more houses to be built in rural areas."
- Anecdotal evidence: "I have witnessed my local area destroyed by an influx of new, poor quality housing."
- Linking phrases: "Moreover, rural building projects often pose a real danger to local wildlife."

Pages 118-119: Component 1

0.1) 1 mark for each valid response given, up to a maximum of five marks. Answers might include:
- It's by the sea.
- It's hidden under mist.
- It has hills covered in bushes.
- The bush-covered hills are at the back of the bay.
- There are paddocks.
- There are bungalows.
- There's a sandy road.
- The paddocks and the bungalows are on the other side of the sandy road.
- There are white dunes covered with reddish grass.
- A heavy dew had fallen.
- There is silvery, fluffy toi-toi grass.
- There are marigolds/pinks/fuschias/nasturtiums in the bungalow gardens.

0.2) All your points should use relevant examples and terminology, and comment on the effects of the language used. Here are some things you could mention:
- The description goes from the calm tone of the sea to the more energetic tone of the fast-flowing, which means the passage builds up in activity, making the "silence" at the end more dramatic.
- The writer uses language to reinforce this build-up. They use the adverb "softly" to describe the sea, giving the start of the passage a calm tone. The writer then introduces more movement with the repetition of "rippling" when describing the sea. The energetic tone is added to by the use of several active verbs, for example "flowing" and "slipping".
- The writer uses sound to help the reader imagine the bay. The alliteration of the 's' sound in "sounded the sleepy sea" and "slipping between the smooth stones" is onomatopoeic, which gives the reader a vivid impression of the gentle, dreamlike atmosphere of the bay, and helps them to imagine being surrounded by the soft noises of the scene.

0.3) All your points should use relevant examples and terminology, and comment on the effects of the language and structure used and its influence on the reader. Here are some things you could mention:
- Descriptive verbs such as "huddled" are used to suggest that the sheep are fearful. This is reinforced by the words used to describe their movements: the sheep "trotted along quickly" as if in fear.

- In contrast the writer presents the dog as unafraid and even nonchalant. It runs along "carelessly", suggesting it is "thinking of something else". This makes the roles of the animals clear to the reader: the dog is a working pet, whilst the sheep are animals in captivity.
- The writer uses imagery to give fine details of how the shepherd looks: his coat is "covered with a web of tiny drops". This detail helps to give the reader a clear picture of the shepherd.
- The entrance of the shepherd is described using a shorter, less detailed sentence than those that surround it ("And then in the rocky gateway the shepherd himself appeared"). This makes his entrance seem dramatic, which emphasises his authority. This is further shown by his actions: "taking his time", he gently whistles a tune. The effect of this is to show the reader that the shepherd is in total control of what he does.

0.4) All your points should use relevant examples and terminology, and comment on the effects of the language and structure used and their influence on the reader. Here are some things you could mention:
- The writer uses the viewpoint of an omniscient third-person narrator to make these lines vivid and interesting. The narrator takes the reader on a journey along the "sandy road" with the shepherd, which allows the writer to relate the effect of the mist, gradually revealing the scene. For example, the "shock-haired giant" that the narrator describes becomes a "big gum-tree". This vivid image helps the narrator to show what the scene looks like, and adds interest for the reader on an emotional level: the reader feels the moment of panic and confusion when something unclear appears through the mist.
- The writer vividly describes the dispersal of the mist using a succession of verbs: the mist "thinned", "dissolved" and "rolled". These verbs are combined in one long sentence to create the effect of a hurried and confused retreat.
- This effect is confirmed by the personification the writer uses: the mist was "in a hurry to escape". Images like these help the reader to more clearly imagine the complex and tumultuous sight of the mist rapidly retreating before the rising sun.

0.5) Your answer should evaluate the text by giving an opinion on the statement. It should comment on the techniques the writer has used to make the scene and characters believable, using relevant examples and terminology to support each point. Here are some things you could mention:
- The writer successfully creates a believable scene because they go beyond visual description, involving senses such as smells and sounds, for example "the smell of the leaves" and "Myriads of birds were singing". This gives the reader a more complete picture of the journey through the bay early in the morning.
- The writer successfully creates a believable character in the dog through her description of his actions, which reveal his personality. The writer gives an insight into what the dog is thinking by describing how he "waggled past" without looking up, showing he was trying to ignore Florrie. The text does this throughout with the dog, for example in an earlier paragraph, the dog's loyalty to the shepherd is revealed as he walks "a few dignified paces by his master's side". This description of the dog's behaviour at different points gives him a developed personality, as he displays a range of emotions like a real animal. This helps to make the character more believable for the reader.
- The shepherd's personality isn't developed in the same way, which could make him seem less believable to a reader. Although earlier in the text details of his physical appearance are given — a "grave, fine-looking old man" — by this last section of the text, he remains nameless, still being referred to as "the shepherd". This makes it hard to know what he thinks and feels, making him a less believable character.

Answers

1.1) Answers need to be entertaining for a general, adult audience. They need to use interesting language techniques to create a suitable tone and style. Writing needs to be well-organised, clear and technically accurate. These answers are for option (b), 'The Misty Morning.' Here are some techniques you could include:

- An interesting, dramatic opening sentence: "The mist appeared too suddenly for them to avoid it."
- Direct address: "If you'd seen what I saw on that misty October morning, you'd have done the same thing."
- Similes: "Just past the end of the jetty, waiting like a promise, was the little red boat."
- Contrasting descriptions: "A brisk, fresh winter breeze began to blow, rapidly clearing the clammy tendrils of stagnant fog."

Pages 123-124: Component 2

1.1) a) They first met at university.
   b) She rang at 6pm.
   c) They might be 70.

1.2) All your points should use relevant examples and terminology, and comment on the effects of the language and structure used and their influence on the reader. Here are some things you could mention:

- Jenni Russell has structured her article to support her assertion that friends are important. At the start, she uses an example to demonstrate the negative effects that friends can have: Jo's loss of her "confidante" was "one of the worst things" she'd ever experienced. Russell then finishes the article with the suggestion that friendship is worth it: people "live longer and are happier" with close friends. This structure allows her to show the reader that she understands the complexities of friendship, so they would be more likely to trust her view that friends are important.

- The writer uses language to relate to the reader and create a friendly, inclusive tone. In the penultimate paragraph, she repeats the pronoun "we". The effect of this is to make the reader feel as if the writer shares and understands the problems that readers have, so they would be more likely to listen to and trust her.

1.3) a) Because he doesn't have any friends.
   b) Because he's afraid that he will see someone who wants to borrow money from him during the daytime.
   c) Susan.

1.4) Your answer should evaluate the text by giving an opinion on it. It should comment on the techniques the writer has used to convey his views on his Boisterous Friend, using relevant examples and terminology to support each point. Here are some things you could mention:

- Wilkie Collins shows that he finds his Boisterous Friend annoying by using animal imagery to describe his behaviour: his laugh is described as a "roar" and he "rushes in like a mad bull". These descriptions help the reader to sympathise with Collins's viewpoint, as they make his friend's behaviour seem out of control.
- The reader may feel that Collins is being overly harsh on his friend. They have known each other since they were children and the Boisterous Friend loves him "like a brother", yet Collins says that he could "dispense" with him. This could make the reader feel that Collins is being ungenerous to his friend.

- However, he does not ultimately "dispense" with his friends, as is shown by him allowing his friend in at the end. As such, it seems likely that his annoyance with his Boisterous Friend is at least partly affectionate. Readers may therefore find his views amusing as they may relate them to similar friends that they have.

1.5) Answers should use relevant quotes or examples from both texts to clearly answer the question. Here are some things you could mention:

- Both writers show that relationships with other people can interfere with your own plans. Russell's friend Jo had planned to go to the cinema, but her plan was disrupted by Genevieve cancelling on her. Collins is planning to go home to finish writing an article, but thinks that he may not have "a clear five minutes" to do so because of interruptions from his friends.
- Wilkie Collins shows that relationships can be problematic because people may try to use you. For example, he writes about his friend who borrows money from him and how he is an "obvious nuisance".
- Russell shows that it "isn't easy" to maintain friendships and that losing a friend can be emotionally distressing. Her friend Jo's experience of losing a friend was "one of the worst things" that had ever happened to her.

1.6) Answers should clearly compare the different attitudes and techniques in each text, using quotations to support points. Here are some things you could mention:

- Collins seems to find friendship tiresome: the way he lists the friends he could "dispense" with in the penultimate paragraph emphasises his desire to part with them. Russell, in contrast, believes that there are "powerful reasons" for maintaining friendships. The word "bonds" suggests that she feels friendships are strong ties that should not be broken.
- Collins is writing satirically. His terms of familiarity, such as "dear", hint at a true fondness for his friends, and his complaint that one friend "never does" ask him to dinner could imply that he does want to socialise, which suggests that he has a positive attitude towards friendship after all. Russell, in contrast, writes with an earnest tone to offer a genuine answer to her title question: "What are friends for?" Readers might be amused by Collins's article, whilst Russell is aiming to share her thoughts and potentially inspire readers to work hard at their friendships.

2.1) Answers need to reflect form, purpose and audience using suitable vocabulary and language techniques. Writing needs to be well-organised, clear and technically accurate. Here are some techniques you could include:

- Formal vocabulary: "It is often perceived that new students suffer most from a lack of confidence."
- Facts and figures: "For 7 out of 10 new students the main difficulty was a lack of openness from existing pupils."
- Clear, direct language: "Firstly, we must educate existing students in the need to be welcoming to newcomers."
- A serious tone: "The importance of this transition period cannot be underestimated."

2.2) Answers need to reflect form, purpose and audience using suitable vocabulary and language techniques. Writing needs to be well-organised, clear and technically accurate. Here are some techniques you could include:

- Conversational style: "I think the writers of this proposal need to take a good, long look at themselves."
- Rhetorical techniques: "Who on Earth actually believes that this can be achieved?"
- Direct address: "I invite you (and all readers) to carefully consider your opinion on this proposal."
- A list of three: "This proposal is old-fashioned, restrictive and deeply unpopular."

Glossary

alliteration	When words that are <u>close together</u> start with the <u>same sound</u>. E.g. "the <u>b</u>eat of the <u>b</u>and".
analogy	A <u>comparison</u> to show how one thing is <u>similar</u> to another, making it easier to <u>understand</u> or more <u>memorable</u>. E.g. "watching cricket is about as much fun as watching paint dry."
antithesis	A technique where <u>opposing</u> words or ideas are presented <u>together</u> to show a contrast.
audience	The <u>person</u> or <u>group of people</u> that read or listen to a text.
biased writing	Gives <u>more support</u> to one point of view than to another, due to the writer's <u>own opinions</u>.
broadsheet	A more <u>formal</u> type of newspaper, which often focuses on more <u>serious</u> topics. E.g. *The Guardian* or *The Telegraph*.
clause	Part of a sentence that has a <u>subject</u> and a <u>verb</u>. <u>Main clauses</u> make sense on their own.
colloquial language	<u>Informal</u> language that sounds like ordinary <u>speech</u>.
commentary (newspaper article)	A type of newspaper article that expresses the <u>opinions</u> of the writer on a theme or news event. Also called a <u>column</u>, <u>opinion piece</u>, or editorial.
connotations	The <u>suggestions</u> that words can make <u>beyond</u> their obvious meaning.
counter-argument	The <u>opposite</u> point of view to the writer's own view. This is useful when writing to argue or persuade — first give the counter-argument, then explain why you <u>disagree</u> with it.
direct address	When a writer talks <u>straight to the reader</u>, e.g. "you might recall..."
emotive language	Language that has an <u>emotional</u> effect on the reader.
explicit information	Information that's <u>directly stated</u> in a text.
figurative language	Language that is used in a <u>non-literal</u> way to create an effect, e.g. personification.
first person	A <u>narrative viewpoint</u> where the narrator is one of the <u>characters</u>.
flashback	A writing technique where the scene shifts from the <u>present</u> to an event in the <u>past</u>.
form	The <u>type</u> of text, e.g. a letter, a speech or a newspaper article.
hyperbole	When <u>exaggeration</u> is used to have an <u>effect</u> on the reader.
imagery	A type of <u>figurative language</u> that creates a <u>picture in your mind</u>, e.g. metaphors and similes.
impersonal tone	A tone of writing that <u>doesn't</u> try to directly <u>engage</u> with the reader.
implicit information	Information that's hinted at <u>without</u> being said outright.
inference	A <u>conclusion</u> reached about something, based on <u>evidence</u>. E.g. from the sentence "Yasmin wrinkled her nose at the lasagne", you could <u>infer</u> that Yasmin doesn't like lasagne.
inversion	Altering the <u>normal word order</u> for <u>emphasis</u>, e.g. "On the table sat a hedgehog."
irony	Saying one thing but <u>meaning the opposite</u>.
limited narrator	A narrator who only has <u>partial knowledge</u> about the events or characters in a story.
linear structure	A type of narrative structure that tells the events of a story in <u>chronological</u> order.
list of three	Using <u>three</u> words (often adjectives) or phrases together to create <u>emphasis</u>.

Glossary

metaphor	A way of <u>describing</u> something by saying that it <u>is</u> something else, to create a vivid image. E.g. "His eyes were deep blue pools."
motif	A <u>recurring</u> image or idea in a text.
narrative	Writing that tells a <u>story</u> or describes an <u>experience</u>.
narrative viewpoint	The <u>perspective</u> that a text is written from, e.g. <u>first-person</u> point of view.
non-linear structure	A type of narrative structure that tells the events of a story in a <u>non-chronological</u> order.
objective writing	A <u>neutral</u>, <u>unbiased</u> style of writing which contains <u>facts</u> rather than opinions.
omniscient narrator	A narrator who <u>knows</u> the thoughts and feelings of all the characters in a narrative.
onomatopoeia	A word that <u>imitates</u> the sound it describes as you say it, e.g. 'whisper'.
pace	The <u>speed</u> at which the writer takes the reader through the events in a story.
paraphrase	Describing or rephrasing something in a text <u>without</u> including a direct quote.
parenthesis	A <u>rhetorical technique</u> where an <u>extra</u> clause or phrase is <u>inserted</u> into a complete sentence.
personification	Describing a non-living thing as if it's a <u>person</u>. E.g. "The sea growled hungrily."
purpose	The <u>reason</u> someone writes a text. E.g. to persuade, to argue, to advise, to inform.
register	The specific <u>language</u> used to <u>match</u> writing to the <u>social situation</u> that it's for.
repetition	The technique of <u>repeating</u> words for effect.
rhetoric	Using <u>language</u> techniques (e.g. repetition or hyperbole) to achieve a persuasive <u>effect</u>.
rhetorical question	A question that <u>doesn't need an answer</u>. E.g. "Why do we do this to ourselves?"
sarcasm	Language that has a scornful or mocking tone, often using <u>irony</u>.
satire	A style of text that <u>makes fun</u> of something, often by <u>imitating</u> it and <u>exaggerating</u> its flaws.
second person	A <u>narrative viewpoint</u> that is written as if the <u>reader</u> is one of the <u>characters</u>.
sensory language	Language that appeals to the <u>five senses</u>.
simile	A way of describing something by <u>comparing</u> it to something else, usually by using the words 'like' or 'as'. E.g. "He was as pale as the moon."
slang	Words or phrases that are <u>informal</u>, and often specific to one <u>age</u> group or <u>social</u> group.
Standard English	English that is considered <u>correct</u> because it uses formal features of <u>spelling</u> and <u>grammar</u>.
structure	The <u>order</u> and <u>arrangement</u> of ideas in a text. E.g. how the text begins, develops and ends.
style	The <u>way</u> that a text is <u>written</u>, e.g. the type of language, sentence forms and structure used.
tabloid	A <u>less formal</u> type of newspaper, which often focuses on more <u>sensational</u> topics.
third person	A <u>narrative viewpoint</u> where the narrator remains <u>outside</u> the events of the story, written using words like 'he' and 'she'.
tone	The <u>mood</u> or <u>feeling</u> of a piece of writing, e.g. happy, sad, serious, light-hearted.
viewpoint	The <u>attitude</u> and <u>beliefs</u> that a writer is trying to convey.

ENWS41